BROKEN WINDOWS OF THE SOUL

BROKEN WINDOWS OF THE SOUL

A Pastor and Christian Psychologist
Discuss Sexual Sins and
the Prescription to Heal Them

Arnold R. Fleagle, DMin
Donald A. Lichi, PhD

WingSpread Publishers
Camp Hill, Pennsylvania

WingSpread Publishers
Camp Hill, Pennsylvania

A division of Zur Ltd.

Broken Windows of the Soul
ISBN: 978-1-60066-275-1
LOC Control Number: 2010943070
© 2011 by Arnold R. Fleagle and Donald A. Lichi

Contents

Foreword

Since the onset of the so-called sexual revolution in Western culture, we have driven ourselves a long way down the road of sexual freedom, gaping at the scenery, only to find the road leads to a prison.

My friends Dr. Arnie Fleagle and Dr. Don Lichi favor a prison break and write this to those already imprisoned by sexual sin or to any of us who are curious about the dangers of this road and who may already be driving that way.

The chapters are crystal clear. You always understand what they are talking about. It is plain talk by two very strong men—I know and admire both of them—who do not try to show off their counseling and pastoring skills with technical jargon. All who read *Broken Windows of the Soul* will comprehend its content.

There is also the right balance of warning and

hope in the chapters you are about to read. The book is candid and correct, biblically and clinically. The reader is brought to well-defined options. You will be cautioned in a careful and not condescending way. But you will also feel you can turn this thing around. You can fix the broken windows, to use the authors' vivid analogy.

The warnings come through straight talk and a lot of true stories, mostly about people who believe in our Lord but did not heed the wise cautioning of Scripture and have yet to face their weaknesses. It would seem foolish for any of us to start down this road or any of its side streets without studying the map this book provides.

And maybe the greatest balance in this whole conversation—a conversation that will feel like a talk with a good friend—is the balance between our responsibility and God's strength in us. The authors are very clear about what we must do to turn destructive sexual habits around with very practical steps. Their remedies give hope but also call for self-discipline and seeking help.

But you are unambiguously reminded in this book that every step toward remedy can and should be taken with strong love for our Lord Christ, the Savior, with dependence on His spiritual stamina. Arnie and Don write with spirits that make you want to go there!

I can see a lot of prison breaks as a result of this good book as well as many lives making U-turns on that road down to the prison. Looking back over the landscape of my ministry, I wish I could have given this book to many who sought my counsel in the areas of sexual temptation and failure. In coaching pastors and churches now, and with friends, I will recommend it constantly.

KNUTE LARSON

Knute Larson served as pastor of The Chapel in Akron, Ohio, for more than twenty-five years (1983–2009). He is currently a church consultant for the Great Lakes District of the Evangelical Free Church of America, an associate Bible teacher for RBC Ministries, adjunct faculty for Moody Bible Institute, Trinity International University and Grand Rapids Seminary as well as author of five books.

PREFACE

Do you find your inner life compromised by repeated yielding to sexual temptation? You are not alone. The moral fabric of our culture is being ripped apart as large numbers of men and women are indulging in infidelity, perverted sexuality and pornography. The destructive nature of these practices is leading to ethical chaos, disintegrating marriages, parental confusion and loss of respect for moral leaders. It is becoming increasingly difficult to find any individuals who are healthy and whole in their lifestyle.

The outlook may appear bleak, but we believe there is *hope* for anyone who wants to break free from sexual compromise and have a healthy marriage, a joyful family, meaningful friendships and a significant legacy for future generations to follow, flowing from an authentic relationship with God.

But beware—the path to freedom is not an easy road to follow. The answer to the pervasive influences of a morally broken culture can be found in the regular practice of spiritual disciplines, which transform the heart and result in a life that is well lived and well remembered. These disciplines require effort, but that should be no surprise; anyone who wants to live a real Christian life will face challenges and crosses. The good news is that, when these trials are courageously and resolutely faced, they lead to a life of adventure and achievement.

We will begin this book with a review of the staggering scope of the sexual blight upon our culture and then discuss how you can build a fence at the top of the cliff of temptation so that you don't find yourself trying to repair the wreckage at the bottom. By focusing on avoiding those habits and inclinations that lead to the trap door of sexual sin, you can move beyond just "sin management" and learn to embrace deep character changes that create a fruitful life and a worthy legacy.

Throughout the book we will apply a sociological concept known as "the broken windows theory"—the idea that fixing small problems promptly helps you avoid the larger catastrophes. This principle, when applied to the challenges of temptation and moral breakdown, provides you with a unique opportunity to keep the damage at a minimum and make your long-term future bright.

In his letter to the Ephesians, the Apostle Paul wrote about the spiritual potential in all of us for great moral triumph as well as tragic moral disaster. He framed the contrast with these words:

> Be imitators of God, therefore, as dearly loved children and live a life of love, just as Christ loved us and gave himself up for us as a fragrant offering and sacrifice to God. But among you there must not be even a hint of sexual immorality, or of any kind of impurity, or of greed, because these are improper for God's holy people. (Ephesians 5:1–3)

It is our prayer that we can assist you to live a dynamic Christian life that resonates with the very character of God as you represent your heavenly Father and shine as stars in the darkness that seems to surround us all.

Let's get to work on the broken windows of our souls and the souls we are ministering to, and begin reversing the effects of sexual sin in our own lives, as well as in this badly dilapidated culture.

THE WINDOWS ARE CRACKING

*"If a window in a building is broken and
is left unrepaired,
all the rest of the windows will soon be broken."*
—James Q. Wilson & George L. Kelling

*"Above all else, guard your heart,
for it is the wellspring of life."*
—Proverbs 4:23

Imagine that you are walking down the street with no one else in sight and you notice an abandoned car. The hood is up, there are no license plates and apparently no one could care less about this car. Would you be tempted to help yourself to some free parts? What if you noticed someone else getting away with some tires, a battery or other accessories? Would you be even more tempted to help yourself?

Several years ago Stanford University psychologist Philip Zimbardo took two cars and parked one on a street in affluent Palo Alto, California, and the other in one of the seediest neighborhoods in the Bronx, New York. As part of the experiment he removed the license plates, raised the hoods and abandoned the cars to their fate.[1] Within ten minutes (!) people in the Bronx began helping themselves to parts of the car and within twenty-four hours virtually everything of value had been stripped. Then random destruction began until the entire car was trashed. In contrast, the car in Palo Alto sat unmolested for a week until Zimbardo smashed one of the windows with a sledgehammer. Within a few hours it, too, was totally demolished.

Reflecting on Zimbardo's research, Malcolm Gladwell, author, speaker and staff writer with *The New Yorker*, stated, "Disorder invites even more disorder; a small deviation from the norm can set into motion a cascade of vandalism and criminality. The broken window was the tipping point."[2] *Once one of the windows was broken, and left unattended, soon the entire car was trashed.*

SERIOUS CONSEQUENCES OF SMALL-SCALE NEGLECT

Zimbardo developed what became known as "Broken Windows Theory," which suggested that to reduce or prevent crime and maintain social order, "small" problems must be fixed immediately. Zimbardo's theory held that a little disorder that goes unattended invites even more disorder. On the heels of Zimbardo's experiment, criminologist George Kelling and social scientist James Q. Wilson reported that a broken window in a building left unrepaired soon led to *all* of the windows in the building being knocked out. Why? Damage left ignored sends a message that "no one cares," "no one is in charge," "we can further vandalize with no penalty." Kelling and Wilson found that neglecting even the smallest things led to abandoned property, growing weeds and additional smashed windows.

"FIX THE BROKEN WINDOWS"
In the 1990s New York City mayor Rudy Giuliani decided to test the Broken Windows Theory. His police chief selected two high crime precincts and ordered the police to "fix the broken windows"— that is, zero tolerance for the small crimes like graffiti, public disorder, aggressive panhandling, the window washers at stoplights, fare jumpers at subway stations, public urination, etc. Police arrested petty offenders, cleaned up the neighborhoods and enforced a zero-tolerance policy for violations of public order. They washed the subways of graffiti daily, cracked down on fare beaters and loiterers and made their presence known.[3, 4]

So, what happened as a result?

SURPRISING STATS
Police officers found that one of seven "petty offenders" had an outstanding warrant; one

of twenty had a gun. Arrests for misdemeanors went up 500 percent between 1990 and 1994. As a result, New York City became one of the safest large cities in the country (actually about as safe as Boise, Idaho on a per capita basis). Car thefts were down seventy-one thousand from one hundred fifty thousand. Burglaries fell from two hundred thousand to seventy-five thousand. Homicides decreased to 1970s levels and dropped by one-half since 1990. Every precinct showed double-digit decreases in violent crime.

Inspired by New York City's dramatic results, communities across the country developed "neighborhood watch" programs. A cursory search of "broken windows" on the Internet reveals thousands of applications in communities, schools and businesses.[5, 6, 7]

Some Good News

The good news is that many communities, schools and businesses are finding that when they began to pay attention to the small details, a positive tipping point emerged. When order is visibly restored at the smallest level, a signal is sent out. "This is a community where bad behavior has serious consequences." "If you can't get away with jumping a turnstile into the subway, you'd better not try armed robbery."[8]

Broken Windows of the Soul

You get the idea, right? Of course "broken windows" is a metaphor for the astonishing speed with which societal norms unravel. A single broken window soon attracts people who will smash more windows. After all, breaking windows is fun, isn't it? Pockets of disorder (graffiti, litter, etc.) communicated that authorities could not or would not enforce standards. Soon, law-abiding citizens left and criminal elements moved in.

The concept of "broken windows" has important spiritual applications for you. In his book *The Christian in Today's Culture,* Charles Colson cites the concept of *shalom* (e.g., civility and harmony) as the key preventative to reduce crime. His compelling challenge to the Christian community is to get involved where we live. He notes, "The best way to reduce crime is not to react after the fact with punishments and rehabilitation but to discourage it before it happens by creating an ordered and civil community life."[9]

Colson appeals to the Christian community to put faith into action by fixing "broken windows" in our communities and cites a number of success stories. He believes that

> it is only Christians who have a worldview capable of providing workable solutions to the problems of community life. Thus, we ought to be in the forefront, helping communities take charge of their own neighborhoods.[10]

As you have already guessed, there are a number of spiritual applications of "broken windows."

This book develops the metaphor of "broken windows" and makes practical applications to your life. Specifically, while we talk about dealing with temptation in general, our main focus is on the myriad of sexual temptations you face on a daily basis. Let's be brutally honest. What "broken windows" have you left unrepaired in your life? Have you been guilty of allowing the litter of immorality, loose talk and compromised values remain like unwashed graffiti in your heart? Have you ignored the voice of God's Spirit by allowing selfish independence, sexual temptation and wandering affections to go unattended? Are you sending a message to God's enemy that no one is in charge; no one cares? What are the consequences of small-scale neglect in the neighborhood of your soul?

LET'S GET STARTED

For much of my professional life as a Christian psychologist, I (Don) have ministered to clergy and religious leaders who have had moral failures. I recall hearing one pastor preach a sermon with fervent conviction on the topic of temptation. He exclaimed, "Moral failure usually begins with an urge, thought or idea long before the act." How true! Sadly, I found out that a couple of years later, he had an affair with the church secretary, divorced his wife and abandoned his family and ministry. What he apparently didn't realize was that the cracks of his own urges, thoughts, fantasies and ideas were not quickly repaired.

When one "broken window" was not quickly fixed, more were soon to follow.

So, how do you deal with the "broken window" of besetting sin and/or temptation? It begins with attending to the "small stuff." Most Christian leaders who found themselves experiencing the consequences of a moral failure never dreamed that their flirtation with sin would lead to such devastating consequences.

There is a heavy price for small-scale neglect. Temptation is an example. Think about the time when you have ignored the "broken windows" of small compromises. Apparently dealing with temptation isn't a twenty-first-century phenomenon. The elder Paul reminds the youthful Timothy to "flee the evil desires of youth" (2 Timothy 2:22). Like a broken window, temptation needs to be dealt with when it is still an urge, a thought or an idea.

You may believe that because you struggle with sexual temptation that you are spiritually weak or that you may have a character flaw. Not so! Scripture is quite clear that Jesus was tempted in every sense that we are—and yet without capitulating to sin (see Hebrews 4:15). To be tempted is not sin. It is only when we are drawn away in our temptation and the evil desire is conceived that it gives birth to sin (see James 1:15). We'll talk much more about this later.

HOW TO GET THE MOST OUT OF THIS BOOK

To make this book even more practical for you, we provide personal reflection questions at the end of each chapter. The temptation will be to skip over these and read through the book. If you do that, you will miss some great opportunities for personal spiritual formation and growth. Further, we advise you to share the book and the reflection questions with a trusted friend. Our prayer is that you will begin to take small steps toward healing and victory in the areas the enemy most wants to destroy you. Take a close and personal look at some of the "broken windows" in your own soul. Will you open your heart to what is presented and ask the Holy Spirit to fix the "broken windows of your soul"?

REFLECTIONS ON MY OWN
"BROKEN WINDOWS"

As you go through the remaining chapters in this book, ask yourself the following questions:

1. What are some of the "broken windows" in my life? Pray and ask the Holy Sprit to reveal any lingering cracks in the windows of your soul. List several triggering events that have been particularly bothersome in dealing with temptation.

2. When are "addictive/sinful" cravings most prevalent? When am I most susceptible to temptation? When I am hungry, angry, lonely or tired? Is it when I'm bored, anxious or depressed?

3. What are some specific consequences I would have to face if discovered in a moral failure?

4. List several guards or "ways of escape" I will employ when I am aware of being in a state of temptation. Be specific.

FOR FURTHER READING

Colson, Charles. *The Christian in Today's Culture.* Tyndale House, 2001 (describes "Broken Windows Theory" in an urban setting).

Gladwell, Malcolm. *The Tipping Point: How Little Things Can Make a Big Difference.* Little Brown and Company, 2000.

Rabey, Lois Mowday. *The Snare: Understanding Emotional and Sexual Entanglement.* NavPress, 1994.

Wilkinson, Bruce. *Set Apart: Discovering Personal Victory Through Holiness.* Multnomah Publishers, 1998, 2003.

Wilson, J.Q., and G.L. Kelling. "Broken Windows." *Atlantic Monthly* (March 1982): 29–38.

2

WHAT'S HAPPENED TO THE NEIGHBORHOOD?

"When there's an elephant in the room, introduce him."
—Randy Pausch,
author of *The Last Lecture*

"While people are saying, 'Peace and safety,' destruction will come on them suddenly, as labor pains on a pregnant woman, and they will not escape."
—1 Thessalonians 5:3

We use the expression "the elephant in the room" to refer to a serious issue or problem that is obvious to everyone but is not being acknowledged or addressed. Sexual sins, and in particular the use of pornography, now constitute a *herd* of elephants that can no longer be ignored. The community we live in—the culture that surrounds us—has been compromised by

immoral practices in epidemic proportions. Recent statistics show the widespread breakdown
in sexual attitudes and habits and the resulting
consequences of compromising with evil. From
our experience as a pastor and a counselor, we
can attest to the escalating vulnerability and vic-
timization of people around us who have been
trapped in sexual sin. It is terrifying and tragic.

You are not just a statistic, however; you are
an individual whom God has formed and framed
for a purpose. You may have "taken the bait"
and the hook is cutting and shredding your life.
You may have a family member or friend who is
hooked and you want to help him or her get free.
Either way, you need to be aware of the gravity of
the situation before we can shed some scriptural
and practical light on successful ways to overcome it.

RELATIONAL DEBRIS

One of us (Arnold) has served as a pastor to several church congregations and as a district director
who worked with more than one hundred ninety
pastors and more than eighty congregations. From
these vantage points he has witnessed the debris
of broken relationships across the emotional landscape. It has now reached astronomical proportions
due to the damage inflicted by infidelity, adultery
and such sexual deviations as pornography.

The multitudes of people in counseling over
these issues, the frequency of splintered marriages, the number of guilt-ridden adolescents

and even the encroachment of these sins into the minds and hearts of grade-school children is rising at an alarming pace. This widespread moral breakdown threatens to bring about cultural collapse. As a society and as individuals we need to be aware of the threat and deal decisively with it. As Christians, we need to be ready to minister to our culture and alleviate the inevitable fallout.

CRACKS IN THE CHRISTIAN WALL

As we look at the church today, what do we discover? One might suspect that the Christian community, which teaches and preaches lofty moral values, would be somewhat insulated from sexual addictions. However, by the 1990s the early cracks in the wall were beginning to be observable and traceable.

Promise Keepers did a survey in 1996 at one of their stadium events, that revealed that more than 50 percent of the men in attendance had viewed pornography within one week of the event.[1] In September 2008, a Promise Keepers event was held in Cleveland, Ohio. As reported in *The Plain Dealer,* Cleveland's daily newspaper, "Attendees who participated in a text message survey were asked what was their most difficult challenge. More than *80 percent* of the text messengers said it was *viewing pornography.*"[2]

Younger men are not exempt from pornography. Jason Carroll, an associate professor at Brigham Young University, declared that "nearly nine in ten college men report some level of use;

50 percent report at least weekly use; and one in four reports daily use."[3]

How about Christian women? They would not indulge in pornography—at least not in significant numbers—would they? It may seem difficult to fathom, yet *Today's Christian Woman* magazine in the fall of 2003 reported that 34 percent of their female subscribers admitted to intentionally accessing Internet porn.[4] So much for the age-old adage, "Men are turned on by sight, and women are turned on by touch." If women are looking at trash and if the eyes are the window of the soul, then it is inevitable that their spiritual lives will be severely contaminated.

An even more frightening statistic may be found in the demographics of pastors—the leaders of the Christian church and supposedly the high-water mark of Christian culture. C. Peter Wagner pointed out in *Prayer Shield* that "over the past couple of decades, an alarming number of pastors have dropped out of the ministry for two main reasons: *pastoral burnout* and *sexual immorality*."[5] What percentage of pastors now say that porn is a temptation to them? The winter 2006 issue of *Leadership* reported that *38 percent* of pastors owned up to the struggle.[6] When almost *four out of ten* trained, equipped and church-commissioned leaders are affected by sexual temptation through visual representation, indeed, the moral foundations are collapsing!

Bob Russell, recently retired from the sixteen thousand-member Southeast Christian Church in Louisville, Kentucky, made this discouraging entry in his book *When God Builds a Church*:

> A few years ago a group of us who are privileged to lead large congregations decided to begin gathering annually for the purpose of fellowship and inspiration. We knew we would enjoy the opportunity to share ideas and encourage one another. But each of the last three years, there has been at least one minister who didn't return. In every case it was because of moral failure in the person's life.[7]

One of the most publicized pastoral failures occurred in 2006 when Ted Haggard, president of the National Association of Evangelicals and pastor of New Life Church in Colorado Springs, Colorado, confessed to sexual immorality with a male prostitute. The tentacles of sexual temptation had extended to the highest levels of the American evangelical church.[8]

Another illustration of the havoc wreaked by sexual sin in pastoral marriages is shared by Debra Laaser in her book, *Shattered Vows: Hope and Healing for Women Who Have Been Sexually Betrayed*. She was married to a respected marriage counselor who was also a part-time Christian college professor and interim pastor. The tidal wave hit fifteen years into her marriage when her husband, Mark, was dismissed for initiating sex with several of his clients.[9]

If the devastating grip of sexual addictions and sins is affecting the Christian church, which professes such high values and standards, where will the society as a whole be found? With the advent of the computer, the infiltration of the mind has come right into the office and the home. The place of solitude provides a quiet retreat to engage in the destruction of ethical purity and the chiseling away of loyalty and satisfaction in marriage.

A pastor who attended a "Broken Windows" seminar later sent an e-mail unfolding his difficulty in maintaining his spiritual health and his commitment to his wife. While desiring to stand strong against sexual temptation, he vividly revealed the battle in which he was engaged.

> I don't know why, but for the past three or
> four months I have been under a continual
> barrage of temptations from the enemy that
> seemed relentless. It seemed that everywhere
> I turned, I was having temptation thrown
> at me. Television ads, TV programs, lust-
> ful thoughts and imaginations, memories
> of inappropriate movies and pictures I had
> literally seen decades ago, provocatively
> dressed women, etc., just seemed to come
> at me relentlessly. I am thankful that I have
> never looked at Internet pornography, nor
> been involved in any kind of inappropriate
> relationships. So, I was baffled as to what the
> source of this temptation was and why it was
> and why it kept coming at me over and over

again for such an extended period. . . .

I have seen so many good pastors bite the dust due to immorality and I have pastored in churches immediately following the resignation of the former pastor due to sexual sin, so I realized that "there but for the grace of God go I." On my own, I am very vulnerable, but God is faithful. This leads me to what the Lord showed me in His Word that helped me deal with such things. In 1 Corinthians 10:13, the phrase, "beyond what you can bear" jumped out at me. I suddenly realized that since I have been growing and maturing in the faith for over forty years, I am able to bear much more temptation than I did as a young teenager, because God is faithful! But it also means that I can expect much stronger and more persistent temptation from the enemy. I can't rest on past victories to get me through. I must be reminded of the continual and increasingly stronger attacks from the enemy. Even after thirty-one years of marriage to the greatest woman on earth, I am still vulnerable and very capable of failing if I take off my spiritual armor or let my guard down, even for a moment. So I must daily commit myself to purity and faithfulness to my marriage vows and my relationship to Christ.

The rewards of moral purity are so fantastic! It is wonderful to be able to hold my wife in my arms and look her straight in the eyes and be able to say how glad I am that there has never been anyone else but her in my arms. [*Used with permission but with name withheld*]

This is being narrated by a pastor. Notice that he is no longer a young man and yet there are diverse and sundry temptations coming from various sources and that some memories from decades ago were still plaguing him. You may be in a healthy marriage, but remember, you can be blindsided. Be alert!

Not too long ago a leading national Christian magazine published a tragic account of a nationally known pastor. This best-selling Christian author, now in his eighties, had engaged in adultery. He had fallen and in his descent he carried down with him much of his legacy and testimony. It brings to mind the words of Vance Havner when he prayed, "Lord, don't let me live long enough to do something stupid and that's what I will be remembered for." Thankfully, the pastor who sent the e-mail ended his testimony on a much more successful note!

You may be a church leader, you may publish best-selling books, you may be married for more than thirty years, but you can still fall! However, if you stand firm and strong, you can show others the way, which is really a form of *disciple-making*.

The proliferation of pornography on the Internet in the last dozen years is staggering! In 1998 there were 71,831 pornographic sites. That number grew in 2001 to 311,652 and by 2003 stood at 1.3 million.[10] From 2003 until 2007 the number multiplied to an almost unthinkable 108 million.[11] The Web is clearly a platform for the seeds of pornographic addiction. A computer user does not even have to be searching for such a site because search words and hypertext links that appear to be normal and natural can lead an innocent man or woman into forbidden territory.

How many politicians have sacrificed to attain national office, only to be tripped up by sexual compromise and verifiable failure? How many star athletes have been lured into extramarital affairs? How many church leaders have surrendered their credentials and left their ministries because the warmth of initial flirtation turned into the bonfire of passion and the ashes of a third-degree marital burn? Bruce Wilkerson, in his book on practical holiness entitled *Set Apart*, shared this somewhat humorous but probably noteworthy anecdote:

> In a recent meeting with a group of forty men, I asked what they felt were the three biggest temptations men face today. A man in the first row called out, "Number one, sex; number two, sex; number three, sex!"[12]

IN CRISIS THERE IS OPPORTUNITY

We cannot ignore how God made us! We must acknowledge that a part of our fabric and fiber can be employed for incredible love and passion or harnessed by the enemy for widespread damage and detonation of the relationships and people we most cherish! Serial killer Ted Bundy, in his interview with Dr. James Dobson on the eve of his execution, referenced pornography frequently. One of his most terrifying quotes dealt with the escalating appetite that the addiction creates:

> My experience with pornography that deals on a violent level with sexuality, once you become addicted to it—and I look on this as an addiction—like other kinds of addiction, I would keep looking for more potent, more explicit, more graphic kinds of material. Like an addiction, you keep craving something which is harder, something that gives you a sense of excitement until you reach the point where the pornography only goes so far. You reach that jumping off point where you begin to wonder if maybe actually doing it will give you that which is beyond just reading about it or looking at it.[13]

Christ, in the Garden of Gethsemane, made crystal clear just how vulnerable His disciples were when He warned, "Watch and pray so that you will not fall into temptation. The spirit is willing, but the body is weak" (Mark 14:38). The desensitization of our culture to immoral sexual behavior has made it more difficult to advise and warn the victims. It is like the proverbial cold-blooded frog in a kettle—boiled alive because he did not notice the temperature rising one degree at a time.

This slow breakdown of moral standards leads to nonsensical comments like this one made by former All-Pro Dallas Cowboys lineman Nate

Newton, in response to criticism of sexual behavior: "We've got a little place over here where we're running some whores in and out, trying to be responsible, and we're criticized for that, too."[14] Running a prostitution ring is "trying to be responsible"? Does anybody hear the water boiling?

But there is hope. Just as a single broken window can lead to the collapse of an entire neighborhood, the opposite of this principle is also true: Fixing small things can have a big impact in a neighborhood, in an individual life, in society. In subsequent chapters we will not simply curse the darkness, but seek to light the candles of a renaissance, as we encourage you in the pursuit of a larger Christian life.

Terry Crist has noted that in the Chinese language "the word for *crisis* is composed of two symbols. The top character represents potential danger; the lower conveys hidden opportunity."[15] Though we are in a moral crisis, we can choose to maximize the opportunities that are presented by the stark and serious dilemma it presents and begin to engage the enemies of our society and our souls. If you are battling sexual sin, you do not have to remain in chronic defeat. You and your "neighborhood" can be revitalized.

Questions for Reflection

1. How have sexual influences and temptations escalated in the world in which you live? Do you personally feel more vulnerable to them?

2. Do you know a church leader or pastor who has fallen victim to sexual sins? Were there any warning signs that he or she was in trouble?

3. Have you observed in teenagers or children you associate with a greater preoccupation with sexual issues? Are children you know more or less sexually savvy than you were at that age?

3

HERE COMES THE LANDLORD

"I don't do pop quizzes before breakfast."
—Garfield

*"For you know very well that the day of the Lord will
come like a thief in the night."*
—1 Thessalonians 5:2

A landlord will sometimes make unexpected visits to a rental property to inspect it and make sure it is being maintained. Tenants who want to please the landlord will remember that the owner of the house could come at any time; they will keep the house neat, sweep the porch and make sure the grass is regularly mowed. Tenants who disregard the landlord's authority and neglect the property may be in violation of their lease and find themselves out on the street.

The Scriptures are unambiguous in their insistence that our bodies are not our own after we receive the forgiveness and mercy of Jesus Christ. The Apostle Paul made it crystal clear: "You are *not your own*; you were bought at a price. Therefore honor God with your body" (1 Corinthians 6:19–20). Consider Romans 14:12: "So then, each of us will give an account of himself to God." Our Lord holds all the deeds to our lives. 1 Peter 2:19 exhorts us to be "conscious of God"—in other words, we need to take care of the property we have been entrusted with, because our Creator has made us stewards of our bodies, and He is watching to see if His people will manage the property well.

The Landlord's View of Sexual Sin

How does the Lord, the Landlord of our bodies and souls, as well as of His Body the church, view sexual sins? There is no fog or mist surrounding this issue, because it was a problem even in the church of the first century. The Corinthian church was infected by various strains of sexual immorality, to the point that the Apostle Paul was grieved to announce, "It is actually reported that there is sexual immorality among you, and of a kind that does not occur even among pagans: A man has his father's wife" (1 Corinthians 5:1). Incest was a shocking reality in the young Christian church!

Paul goes on to explain how the offender should have been dealt with: "And you are proud! Shouldn't you rather have been filled with grief and have put out of your fellowship the man who

did this?" (5:2). The Corinthian congregation was
served notice that *expulsion* was the appropriate
penalty for incest within the church body—and
the punishment was long overdue! Paul extends
the discussion and concludes with a summary
that critiques and empowers the church to deal
decisively with those inside its membership:
"What business is it of mine to judge those outside the church? Are you not to judge those inside
[the church]? God will judge those outside. 'Ex-
pel [the same word employed in verse 2, which
means "to lift out"] the wicked man from among
you'" (5:12–13).

In the next chapter Paul expands his argument against sexual sin by declaring,

> "Food for the stomach and the stomach for
> food"—but God will destroy them both. The
> body is not meant for sexual immorality, but
> for the Lord, and the Lord for the body. By his
> power God raised the Lord from the dead, and
> he will raise us also. *Do you not know that your
> bodies are members of Christ himself?* Shall I then
> take the members of Christ and unite them
> with a prostitute? Never! Do you not know
> that he who unites himself with a prostitute
> is one with her in body? For it is said, "The
> two will become one flesh." But he who unites
> himself with the Lord is one with him in spirit.
>
> Flee from sexual immorality. All other sins
> a man commits are outside his body, but he
> who sins sexually sins against his own body.
> (6:13–18)

WHO OWNS OUR BODY

A well-accepted concept in Christian theology is that "God owns all the deeds." This includes the deeds to our bodies as well—we are not the landlords, we are the tenants. Therefore, the improper use of our bodies to engage in sexual immorality is an offense against the Landlord.

A heresy in the early Christian church, gnosticism, held to the idea that the body is evil and the spirit is good; therefore, what we do with the body does not matter. Some Christians today appear to believe this as well. While they claim to desire a spiritual relationship with God, they don't seem to think their relationship with God has any connection to their physical behavior.

Of course, the falseness of gnosticism, both the ancient and modern versions, is easily seen in even a brief look at what Scripture has to say on this subject. When Paul urges believers to "honor God with your body" (1 Corinthians 6:20), he obviously does not think our physical bodies are utterly evil—if they were, how could we honor God with them? And if we *can* honor God with our bodies, it clearly means that how we use our bodies is important.

The care and stewardship of our bodies matter to the heavenly Landlord. The secular culture does not understand—let alone agree with—this concept of divine ownership, but for those who profess and practice Christianity, using our bodies for the glory of God is very significant and redemptive. Paul's teaching on the spiritual consequences of joining with a prostitute—that it is, in effect, the same as joining the Lord's body to a prostitute—has thundering implications for our sexual behavior today. A.T. Robertson framed the thrust of this passage in these terms: "Fornication violates Christ's rights in our body."[1]

In verse 18 Paul issues a strong and nonnegotiable command: "Flee from sexual immorality." There is a moment between the temptation and the response in which we have been given an option, and our choice invokes God's pleasure—or His displeasure. Shakespeare wrote it so elegantly: "There is a tide in the affairs of men, which taken at the flood leads on to fortune: omitted all the voyage of their life is bound in shallows and miseries."[2] Many of these watershed moments occur at the moment of choice—to honor the Lord with our bodies, or offend Him by abusing the God-crafted gift of physical existence.

When the choice is wrong, the devastation is often far and wide. Dr. Robert Traina arrested me in seminary with this thought: "You can choose to jump off a cliff, but you cannot choose the consequences that await you at the bottom." When we jump off the precipice of sexual sin, the consequences are built into our choice.

TWO LIONS

Richard Burr, who has taught on private prayer across America, made this statement: "There are two lions in all of us; whichever one we feed wins!" Paul's letter to the Galatians identifies these two lions:

> So I say, live by the Spirit, and you will not
> gratify the desires of the sinful nature. For the
> sinful nature desires what is contrary to the
> Spirit, and the Spirit what is contrary to the
> sinful nature. They are in conflict with each
> other, so that you do not do what you want.
> (5:16–17)

The two lions competing for our allegiance
are the *spiritual* side of us and the *sinful* side of us.
If the Holy Spirit is driving the vehicle of our behavior and we assume the role of passengers, the
result is a righteous, holy, productive life. If the
sinful nature is having its way and navigating the
course of our lives, the outcome is a broken and
dark existence that dead-ends in a dismal life and
legacy.

The more a man or woman is Spirit-led, the
more his or her ethics are developed and regulat-
ed by the Word of God; the more a person hangs
with the right company, the more that man or
woman will abstain from destructive sexual ten-
dencies and invest in acts and activities that reflect the love and character of Jesus Christ—that
is, a Christian *modus operandi*. To put it another
way, the principle of a Spirit-controlled life can
be compared to that time-honored football principle, "The best defense is a good offense." If you
keep your offense on the field, the other team
does not have an opportunity to score.

In the Galatians 5 passage, this contrast between the Spirit-led nature and the sinful nature is followed up with a litany of dirty laundry—the wardrobe of those who forsake a Christian lifestyle for a self-oriented sinful lifestyle. Paul hangs out these filthy rags for all to see:

> The acts of the sinful nature are obvious: sexual immorality, impurity and debauchery; idolatry and witchcraft; hatred, discord, jealousy, fits of rage, selfish ambition, dissensions, factions and envy; drunkenness, orgies, and the like. I warn you, as I did before, that those who live like this will not inherit the kingdom of God. (Galatians 5:19–21)

Most of us do not start out dreaming of this soiled wardrobe being draped around us! We envision a more noble and significant description of our spiritual portrait. And we should aim much higher than that! It should be noted that Paul's phrase "who live like this" uses an expressive word for a *habitual*, not *sporadic*, practice. Most alarming, however, is the sober verdict included at the end of the passage: those who practice these behaviors are *excluded* from the everlasting kingdom!

As I was writing this paragraph, I received a call from a missionary who shared with me that her marriage had been ruined by the same destructive practices outlined in Galatians 5. Her husband, a former pastor, followed the negative example of his father, who was also engaged in sexual sins. With lament oozing through the phone, she related the destruction that traveled through their family—all because two tempted men fed the wrong lion!

HOLINESS AS A LIFESTYLE

Holiness or *Godlike qualities* are to be the signature of the Christian life. The objective, as Paul puts it, is to *"be* imitators of God, therefore, as dearly loved children and live a life of love, just as Christ loved us and gave himself up for us as a fragrant offering and sacrifice to God" (Ephesians 5:1-2). The apostle continues with this strong word of counsel: "But among you there must not be even a hint of sexual immorality, or of any kind of impurity, or of greed, because these are improper for God's holy people" (5:3). The marred profile of a diseased and defeated believer detracts from God's original design for His kingdom and its holy servants.

God takes His will extremely seriously, and in light of that, consider this passage from what many consider to be the earliest of Paul's letters: "It is God's will that you should be sanctified: that you should avoid sexual immorality" (1 Thessalonians 4:3). Why does Paul virtually *equate* sanctification with avoiding sexual immorality? Because, as he goes on to explain, living a holy life is a matter of self-control: "Each of you should learn to control his own body in a way that is holy and honorable, not in passionate lust like the heathen, who do not know God" (4:4–5). Sexual sins are symptomatic of meager discipline, impetuous passion and short-term gratification!

Paul also warns of the danger of overextending one's emotions relative to his brother or sister: "And that in this matter no one should wrong his brother ["to go beyond" in the original language] or take advantage of ["to take more, to overreach" in the original langage] him. The Lord will punish men for all such sins, as we have already told you and warned you" (4:6). The Landlord becomes the *Avenger* when a person crosses the boundaries of sexual propriety and violates, in a figurative sense, the property of another. This principle is seen in the prophet Nathan's rebuke of David for his sin of adultery with Bathsheba (see 2 Samuel 12:1–14): He compared it to stealing another man's sheep!

John Wesley's mother gave him some crucial counsel:

> Would you judge the lawfulness or the
> unlawfulness of pleasure? Take this rule:
> Whatever weakens your reason, impairs
> the tenderness of your conscience, obscures
> your sense of God, or takes off the relish of
> spiritual things—in short, whatever increases
> the strength and authority of your body over
> your mind—that thing is sin to you, however
> innocent it may appear in itself.[3]

The Landlord is coming to assess the tenant

of His property. Will He find it in good order, or will He find it in sad disrepair? Certainly, He will do His part and we must do ours, so that He will be pleased when He returns—and we will not be found to be the victims of our own sinful and selfish impulses!

QUESTIONS FOR REFLECTION

1. How have you addressed the command to glorify God in your body? Are there any activities you should add to or subtract from your daily schedule to improve in this area?

2. Richard Burr taught that there are two lions in all of us: the Spirit-lion and the flesh-lion, each fighting for supremacy. Whichever one you feed wins! What are some ways you can feed the Spirit-lion?

3. In what ways are you strengthening your mind? How are you setting your mind on things above (see Colossians 3:2)?

4

SPIDERS IN THE GLASS

Sow a thought and you reap an action;
Sow an act and you reap a habit;
Sow a habit and you reap a character;
Sow a character and you reap a destiny.
—Ralph Waldo Emerson

Sheep usually get lost one bite at a time.
—Dallas Willard

Therefore do not let sin reign in your mortal body so
that you obey its evil desires. Do not offer the parts of
your body to sin, as instruments of wickedness, but
rather offer yourselves to God, as those who have been
brought from death to life; and offer the parts of your
body to him as instruments of righteousness.
—Romans 6:12–13

Several years ago, my wife and I (Don) drove the entire Alaska Highway through the Canadian Rocky Mountains headed toward Anchorage where I would complete my final three years in the United States Air Force. We were excited about the adventure and felt that we had prepared our Jeep pickup truck for the long trek over hundreds of miles of gravel highway. We took pains to cover our headlights with plastic overlays, and we mounted a screen to keep rocks from flying into our radiator.

Unfortunately, despite all our precautions, an 18-wheeler speeding in the opposite direction threw rocks into the air, and POP! We had a crack in the windshield. Over time the crack spread and became what is known as a "spider" in the glass.

Before a windshield breaks completely there are usually a small series of cracks in the glass, called "spiders" because they look like a spider's web. Spiders in the glass, if not quickly fixed, compromise the integrity of the windshield. When enough of these tiny fissures compound on the windshield's surface, it only takes a small amount of added pressure to cause the glass to shatter.[1]

Could it be that there are spiders in *your* windshield? The progressive levels of involvement in sexual addiction to pornography, like spiders in a windshield, can severely compromise spiritual integrity. What begins as mere curiosity or unintended exposure to pornography has the potential to build into a serious addiction. Let's take a look at how these spiders start to develop in the windows of the soul and how they need to be fixed quickly and preemptively.

GOD'S DESIGN OF THE BODY'S PLEASURE SYSTEM

The body is uniquely designed by God to seek out pleasure and avoid pain. We bond to things that are good and stay away from things that are harmful—and this instinctive reaction is one of God's greatest gifts. A simple example is the bonding that takes place between a baby and its mother through feeding, diapering, rocking, caressing and crooning. In healthy families, the child's pleasure experiences outweigh the painful ones. Later, the child forms attachments to others in the family and to an expanded social network of friends.

Similarly, our relationship with God should provide our greatest pleasure (see Psalm 16:11). As Dr. Richard Dobbins notes, "A joyful relationship with God protects us from coming under bondage to some counterfeit source of pleasure and satisfaction."[2] Whatever you feed tends to grow, and habits are formed by repetitive behavior.[3]

Our brains have a built-in reward mechanism that binds the memory of a pleasurable experience to the source of that pleasure. If our primary pleasure bonds are not formed with the Lord and other loved ones, we will inevitably be brought under the destructive bondage to substitute sources of pleasure. No wonder the Holy Spirit instructs the Corinthian church to "flee"—run away!—from sexual sins. They are not only alluring, they are also addictive and destructive.

The pervasive and pernicious aspects of sexual addiction caught our attention at EMERGE Ministries as we worked with an alarming number of clergy who experienced moral failure. Why is this type of sin so prevalent and innately destructive?

One must first recognize that there are physical (neurological), emotional, chemical and spiritual elements to the addictive progression. The difficulty of dealing with sexual addiction is that it taps into three major areas problematic in any addiction. For example, in most addictions, an "arousal"-prone person will be drawn to stimulants. A "fantasy"-prone person will likely prefer hallucinogens. A "relaxation"-prone person prefers opiates, barbiturates and depressants, such as alcohol. The alarming discovery we made was that pornography uniquely taps into all three of these dimensions. There is the anticipation (arousal), the fantasy (hallucinogen) and following an orgasmic experience, one achieves the relaxation (opiate/depressant) effect.[4]

Consider just a couple of quotes from a U.S. Senate hearing on the addictive nature of pornography:

> It is time to quit regarding porn as just another form of expression because it wasn't.

The eye is a very carefully designed delivery system for evoking a tremendous flood within the brain of endogenous opioids. Modern science allows us to understand that the underlying nature of an addiction to pornography is chemically nearly identical to a heroin addiction. (Jeffrey Satinover, MD)

That [pornographic] image is in your brain forever. If that was an addictive substance, you, at any point for the rest of your life, could in a nanosecond draw it up [and get high]. (Mary Anne Layden, PhD, University of Pennsylvania Center for Cognitive Therapy)[5]

We initiated a thorough search of the brain/mind/addiction literature and also worked with a major religious denomination to establish scales that would measure levels of involvement with porn.[6, 7] The denomination adopted the "levels of involvement" to assist in various levels of ministry suspension and treatment requirements.

The following "stages" would be a good starting point to determine and assess the "spiders" in the glass of your soul. It is important to identify these habits, and deal with them promptly, no matter what stage you may find yourself in. Because pornography taps into all three of the major areas of addiction, one can move quite quickly (in a matter of days) from the "curiosity" stage to the "addictive" stage.

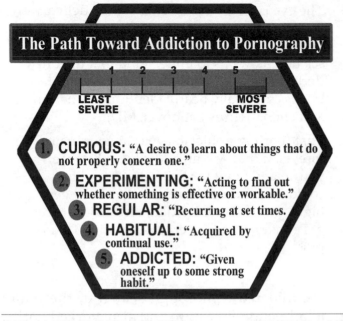

The Path Toward Addiction to Pornography

1 2 3 4 5

LEAST SEVERE   MOST SEVERE

1. **CURIOUS:** "A desire to learn about things that do not properly concern one."

2. **EXPERIMENTING:** "Acting to find out whether something is effective or workable."

3. **REGULAR:** "Recurring at set times."

4. **HABITUAL:** "Acquired by continual use."

5. **ADDICTED:** "Given oneself up to some strong habit."

Definitions are from Webster's New World Dictionary of the American Language, Second College Edition. David B. Guralnik, Editor-in Chief. New York: Simon and Schuster, Inc. 1986

Model © 1998 Dr. Richard D. Dobbins Akron, Ohio. All Rights Reserved

Model by EMERGE Ministries and The Assemblies of God

CURIOUS

1. Have tended to engage in conversation that makes liberal use of sexual innuendo or double entendres

2. Have preferred humor that has strong sexual content or suggestive overtones

3. Find it difficult to maintain eye contact rather than staring at the body of an attractive member of the opposite sex

4. Have been aware of staring at members of the opposite sex to see if the outline of undergarments could be seen

5. Find it difficult, when interacting with attractive members of the opposite sex, not to think about what they might look like unclothed or imagine them being sexual with you

6. Have "surfed" through television shows looking for those with the most suggestive sexual content

7. Have tuned to cable TV channels with scrambled signals to see if nudity or pornography (sights or sounds) was discernible

8. When in convenience stores or similar businesses, have scanned the magazine racks for glimpses of sexually oriented material

EXPERIMENTING

1. Searched for pornography using an Internet Web search engine

2. Have entered an adult-oriented chat room on the Internet

3. Have reviewed pornographic books or magazines in a store

4. Have rented an X-rated DVD/video/movie or purchased other sexually explicit materials

5. Have gone into an "adult entertainment"/ strip club

6. Have masturbated while involved with (or soon after) pornography/sexually oriented Internet contacts

7. Felt guilty for involvement with pornography

8. Felt tempted to use pornography after argument with romantic partner

REGULAR

1. Have accessed sexual sites on the Internet from computers besides those in home
2. Have sexual sites on Internet bookmarked
3. Have several places/sites that are checked frequently to see if material has been changed/ updated
4. Have joined sexual sites on the Internet to gain access to online sexual material
5. Have spent money for sexually oriented materials or interaction at pay sites on the Internet
6. Found it necessary to find new sexual material or contacts after losing interest in previously viewed pornography or online interactions
7. Have feared being caught in inappropriate sexual activities
8. Have developed ways to avoid being caught or detected being involved in pornography
9. Have been secretive/lied about involvement with pornographic activities or time spent involved in them
10. Have been caught looking at or participating in pornography or with sexually oriented material on a computer
11. Have stayed up late (after others have gone to bed) in order to participate in pornography
12. Pornographic use has interfered with work effectiveness (e.g., tired or tardy due to being up late with pornography the night before, using work time to engage in pornographic activities)
13. Spent time with pornographic materials or online sexual interactions during time that could

be better spent with family or friends

14. Have fantasized about pornographic materials while having sexual interactions with a partner

15. Gone significant periods of time without involvement in pornographic materials only to be drawn back into it from time to time

16. Have made promises to self and/or others to stop use of pornographic material and later broken the resolution

17. Have used pornography to reduce/relieve anger, stress, tension, sadness or other uncomfortable emotional states

18. Have used pornography as a reward for achievement or hard work

HABITUAL

1. Regularly buy or have a subscription to sexually oriented materials

2. Spend more than five hours per week using computer for sexual pursuits or engaging in other pornographic activities

3. Spent more time than intended with pornography or cybersex

4. Been upset with self for "wasting time" with pornographic material

5. Have diminished or quit other leisure/recreational activities to spend time with pornographic activities

6. When not engaged in pornographic activities, find self daydreaming or thinking about next opportunity to participate in them again

7. Have felt anxious, angry and/or disappoint-

ed when something interferes with plans to access pornographic activities

8. Do not feel "normal" when attempting to avoid use of pornography (e.g., more depressed or irritable)

9. Have tried to stop inappropriate activities by doing things like throwing away pornography, deleting sexually oriented bookmarks and files or avoiding businesses that handle sexually explicit materials but find it difficult to maintain consistent success

10. Have found a need/desire to be involved with materials/interactions of an increasingly graphic nature to attain the same level of sexual excitement

11. Have been told by others about their concern for your involvement with pornographic material

12. Have been irritable or angry with others when confronted about use of pornography

13. Have been disciplined at work for using company time and/or equipment to procure or engage in pornographic activity

14. Use of/involvement with pornography has had detrimental effects on relationships with spouse, family and/or friends

15. Exposure to pornography has developed interests in sexual activities that are beyond what is comfortable for your romantic partner

16. Secretly worry that behavior with pornographic material is out of control

ADDICTED

1. Have neglected important responsibilities (e.g., absenteeism, missed appointments, diminished work effectiveness, late or missed family functions, etc.) due to involvement with pornographic activities

2. Have accumulated credit card debt (more than what could be paid off at the end of the billing cycle) or spent money on pornography that was budgeted for other things

3. Have lost a job due to involvement with pornography intruding on work performance

4. Have lost important friendships or family relationships due to the use of pornography

5. Have been concerned about possible physical harm or medical problem as a result of excessive masturbation or other sexual activity related to pornography

6. Have risked exposure to disease or injury to engage in pornographic activity

7. Despite important/significant losses, continue to be involved with pornographic activities

8. Feel desperate/hopeless that involvement with pornography could be stopped

9. Find it easier to be sexually involved with pornography than with romantic partner

10. Have accessed illegal material (e.g., child pornography) or engaged in fantasy acts or experiences online that would be illegal if carried out in real life (e.g., rape, voyeurism, exhibitionism, etc.)

11. Have responded to or placed an ad online

or in a sexually oriented publication to solicit involvement in pornographic activity

12. Have acted out sexually with someone you became acquainted with through pornography

13. Believe yourself to be a sex addict

Another important resource to help determine if you might be addicted to pornography is provided by Patrick J. Carnes, who serves as clinical director of Sexual Disorder Services at The Meadows in Wickenburg, Arizona. He developed an anonymous "Internet Sex Screening Test," which is available for those concerned about their Internet sexual behavior.[8]

Having frankly and systematically assessed your own (private) sexual behavior, have you allowed "spiders" to develop in the window of your soul? You must guard your own heart. Don't forget that God's enemy has already established a strategic plan to ruin your life, family and ministry. He hates God, and he hates you as God's prized and redeemed possession.

QUESTIONS FOR REFLECTION

1. Do the self-assessment based on the various levels or "stages" of pornography use. Be completely honest. Where are you?

2. Consider completing Carnes' Internet pornography test and compare your responses to others.

3. What are you willing to acknowledge about your involvement and compromises?

4. If you find that you have gone beyond the curiosity stage, what is your plan to break the pattern before it becomes an addiction?

5

TRIPLE-PANED INSULATION

Above all else, guard your heart, for it is the
wellspring of life.
—Proverbs 4:23

When it comes to saving energy thanks to better home
insulation, a triple-pane window is among the very
best choices. The point is to stop all that heat from
transferring to the outside straight through the win-
dows, and a triple-pane window can do just that. . . .
A window with three panes is an investment rather
than a purchase. . . .
Three panes of glass mean six surfaces of windowpane
. . . . There are also insulation benefits to triple-glass
windows because of the two internal fill spaces rather
than just one as in double paned. These spaces are
filled with air, argon or sometimes krypton and work
to stop heat transfer, as well as cutting down on noise.[1]
—Anthony Lee

How does a person guard his or her heart and thereby build a shelter and preserve a godly legacy for himself?

I (Don) recall a conversation with Dr. Michael Easley, former president of Moody Bible Institute, in which he opened his Bible to reveal a specific list of consequences he would personally experience if he were to give in to a moral failure. He noted such things as the disappointment and pain he would bring to his family. He pointed out those who had invested in his life since he was a boy and how disappointed they would be at the news of his transgression. He noted the loss of ministry and effectiveness for the kingdom of God that he would forfeit. Then he turned to the back of his Bible and said he was keeping a running list of ministry colleagues who had experienced moral failures. He noted sadly that the list was growing at an alarming rate.

One of the guards against sexual sin suggested by Rev. Knute Larson, former senior pastor of the Chapel in Akron, Ohio, was to develop a "master schedule" or an "ideal week." He noted how important it was to keep a healthy balance in ministry that included more or less scheduled time for devotional time, physical exercise, study, visitation, staff meetings, family time and a day off.

If you are engaged in ministry, it is important not to confuse your *work for* God with your *walk with* God. It is possible, at least for a brief period of time, to be successful in your *work* while a failure in your *walk*. However, just as a window with cracks eventually breaks, so it is with our heart and soul. It is only a matter of time until one experiences burnout, discouragement and the vulnerability of a moral failure.

Remember that the premise of "broken windows" is that disorder invites even more disorder. It is important to take care of the faults, foibles and small behavioral blemishes in your life so that you are far less likely to have to deal with the big ones later on. We have seen large-scale consequences borne of small-scale neglect in our communities, churches, schools, homes and families.

But what about the heart's role in the battle against the sins that assail us? Is there any question as to the importance God places on the heart? God emphasizes the priority of guarding our hearts with the phrase "above all else" (Proverbs 4:23). And it is ultimately *our* responsibility—the understood subject of the phrase is "you." The action verb is "guard." What is your plan to insulate and guard your heart against the unrelenting temptations that plague men and women on a regular basis?

We know from the last chapter that the winds of pornography blow against the windows of our souls. We must build up a triple pane of insulation to guard our own heart.

The heart is the residence of God, and it also holds the treasures of life. Everything we value in life is found in the heart. This is why the Bible calls our heart the wellspring of life. Whatever we feed grows and flourishes. Practicing the spiritual disciplines provides fuel for the fire of the Holy Spirit.

THE ENEMY'S STRATEGIC PLAN

Do you know that the enemy has already developed a strategic plan to ruin your life? You need to develop a defensive plan to counter his schemes. If you've ever had training in strategic planning, you're probably familiar with the SWOT principle—the importance of doing a self-assessment of your Strengths, Weaknesses, Opportunities and Threats—as a way of laying the groundwork for a successful plan. For our purposes, let's start with the "W" in SWOT: weaknesses.

When are you most vulnerable to temptation? At EMERGE Ministries we have found that those in ministry are most vulnerable to the enemy's attacks when the following are in place:

- When they have not spent much time alone with God
- When they have not had enough rest
- When life is difficult
- During times of change
- After a significant victory
- When life is going relatively smoothly
- When they are physically exhausted and tired
- When they are discouraged or "down"
- When they are spiritually depleted or "empty"
- When they feel distant or alone
- When they feel internally hopeless or sad

- When they feel insecure or unsure of themselves
- When they have allowed bitterness or anger to fester
- When they feel "wounded" or hurt
- When they feel taken advantage of, taken for granted or unappreciated

In other words, pastors and ministry leaders (much like the rest of us) are most susceptible to sexual sin, as the "twelve-step" people are fond of saying, when they are Hungry, Angry, Lonely or Tired (HALT).

INSTALLING A TRIPLE-PANE WINDOW TO CARE FOR YOUR HEART

How can you care for your heart? You need to make it a daily habit to guard your heart against Satan's attacks. It must be a top priority, especially in light of the "broken windows" principle that small-scale neglect has long-term consequences.

Why should you guard your heart? It is God's command. Guarding your heart helps protect and develop your relationship with Him. A guarded heart provides a pure and clean spiritual environment for the Holy Spirit to function in your life. Finally, caring for your heart is an act of obedience showing God your love and faith in Him.[2]

You will be all the more motivated to follow the command when you consider that God knows exactly how to take care of your heart. He knows what you need and when you need it. A good starting point to guarding your heart is simply to ask God to show you the things in your life that are "broken" and that harm your relationship with Him. Of course, to do this, your relationship with God needs to be deep enough that you are able to understand and practice the things He reveals to you.[3]

Jesus modeled the proper care of the heart. He often took the time even from His messianic ministry to be alone with the Father in silence, solitude and prayer: *"Very early in the morning, while it was still dark,* Jesus got up, left the house and went off to a solitary place, where he prayed" (Mark 1:35).

THE NATURE OF TEMPTATION

It is important to remind ourselves that to be tempted is *not* a sin. Jesus was tempted "in every way, just as we are—yet was without sin" (Hebrews 4:15). Further, we are reminded in Scripture that "no temptation has seized you except what is common to man. And God is faithful; he will not let you be tempted beyond what you can bear. But when you are tempted, he will also provide a way out so that you can stand up under it" (1 Corinthians 10:13).

The devil, however, is a subtle foe; temptation typically comes upon us before we are consciously aware of it. That is the point at which the Holy Spirit warns us and provides "a way out," as the verse above puts it. Nevertheless, it is vital to remember that temptation needs to be dealt with as early as possible, when it is still an urge, thought, fantasy or idea. When ignored, temptation tends to intensify to the point that if we do not immediately take the Spirit's way of escape, we will be led to begin acting out—with the inevitable consequences.

A MODEL TO PUT OFF THE OLD SELF AND PUT ON THE NEW SELF[4]

"You were taught, with regard to your former way of life, to put off your old self, which is being corrupted by its deceitful desires; to be made new in the attitude of your minds; and to put on the new self, created to be like God in true righteousness and holiness" (Ephesians 4:22–24).

The believer's character, spiritual growth, reputation and kingdom effectiveness are a consequence and outgrowth of life choices he or she makes over time. We continually make behavioral choices in response to:

1. Jesus Christ
2. Our old nature
3. Direct temptation from God's enemy

By choosing to respond to Jesus, our divine potential for Christian growth and maturity is enhanced. By choosing to respond to our old nature (old habits) or to God's enemy, our spiritual growth is stymied and our effectiveness for God's kingdom is diminished. At EMERGE Ministries, we have developed a model called "Putting Off the Old Self . . . Putting On the New Self," which presents a practical way to help counselees respond to temptation.

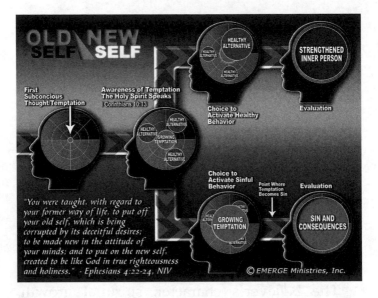

An important step toward victory over temptation is learning to identify the "triggering mechanisms"—those things that spark the thoughts that lead to behavioral choices. Temptation always begins in the mind: Our spiritual battles are won or lost in the four inches between our ears. This is where spiritual warfare really takes place.

Another thing to consider is that the periods of time when we are relatively free of temptation are clearly few and far between. Consider that a good speaker can talk at about 450 words per minute—but our thoughts race along at up to *ten times* that speed! That means we have the potential to experience temptation several thousand times a day.

Most temptations are likely to begin even before we are conscious of them. Then there is a

brief time between the first awareness of tempting thoughts and the loss of control over them.
This period is represented on the diagram as a
"growing temptation," which is accompanied by
an awareness of healthy alternatives (the "way
out" provided by the Holy Spirit; see 1 Corinthians 10:13).

The first awareness of being tempted may
be accompanied by an urge, thought, fantasy
or idea. Triggering influences may be a mood, a
place, a certain person, etc. Bear in mind, God is
always faithful to provide both a warning and a
way of escape whenever we are tempted.

Remember, temptation in and of itself is *not*
sin! One of the most common lies of the enemy is, "No real Christian would ever have such
thoughts! You might as well give in; you've lost
the battle already." The devil will whisper that in
your ear as soon as you begin to resist his entice-
ments.

If we ignore the warning signs and way of escape that God the Holy Spirit suggests, we follow
the path shown in the lower part of the diagram
and eventually lose control over the increasing
power of temptation. At some point, we act out
the "old self" and sin. This leads to self-condem-
nation and shame, and we lose ground in our
spiritual maturing process.

Some believers have lost days, weeks, even
years of spiritual growth, to say nothing of the
erosion of their character, the damage to their
reputation and the injury to their Christian tes-

timony. In some cases (the story of David and Bathsheba, to give just one example), the choice to yield to sin can have devastating and irreversible consequences for the person who sinned—and for others.

However, if we wisely listen to the promptings of the Holy Spirit and choose a healthy alternative behavior (the path shown in the upper part of the diagram), we are strengthened in the inner person. We make progress in our spiritual maturity and experience the pleasure and holiness of God.

The enemy wants to blind us to the consequences of our choices. One of the wisest things we can do in response to temptation is to carefully consider the natural and logical outcomes of the choices placed before us. As one popular humorist said, "If you don't want to go to Minneapolis, *don't get on the train!*"

A good Christian counselor can often help you identify the triggering mechanisms of temptation and come up with healthy substitute behaviors. If you respond quickly to the urges of the Holy Spirit, these small victories will, over time, sow into the soil of your life behaviors that lead to a harvest of holy habits, godly character and a glorious eternal destiny!

TRIPLE-PANE INSULATION: THE THREE SKILLS

There are three skills—the triple-pane insulation in the window of your soul—which, with

God's help, you must develop to effectively counter temptations of thought:

First, you must *identify the triggering mechanisms for such thoughts*. Ask the Holy Spirit to help you become aware of those things that open the door of your mind to temptation. As we said before, a trigger can be a mood, a place, certain persons, etc.

For example, if you find that temptations most often occur when you are alone and unoccupied, avoid being alone as much as possible, or be sure that when you are alone, you plan for it with a healthy activity to keep your mind occupied. I find businessmen to be particularly susceptible to sexual temptation when they are away on business trips and alone (and lonely) in their hotel rooms.

Some believers are most likely to be tempted, ironically, after a great spiritual victory. A spiritual high can often be followed by a period of physical or emotional exhaustion in which we let our defenses down. After a big success, we may also feel "entitled" to indulge in sinful behavior, because we have done so many great things for the Lord.

If a particular part of town or a certain kind of place sets off tempting thoughts, plan your travel route to avoid those places. If that is not possible, have some type of accountability system in place. Perhaps your spouse or a close friend can be "on call" to help you through a difficult period. Scripture is clear that we are to "avoid every kind of evil" (1 Thessalonians 5:22), and 1 Corinthians 6:18 commands us to "flee from sexual immorality."

It may take several days or weeks to identify all the triggers you are prone to, but it is important for you to uncover these hidden traps of the enemy. Otherwise, he will take advantage of your spiritual blindness and defeat you.

The second skill one must develop in using this practical model for putting off the old self and putting on the new self is that of *implementing substitute behaviors*. Once you realize you are being tempted, turn your attention to some activity that will remove you mentally, emotionally and spiritually from the temptation. For example, when a man realizes he is being tempted by what is on the television, computer or video, he may need to practice turning it off and picking up a good book.

Third, because temptation thrives on secrecy, a habit you need to develop is *sharing your struggle*. Go to your spouse or a trusted friend when you first are tempted. Share the secret with him or her, and have him or her pray with you. James 5:16 says, "Confess your sins to each other and pray for each other so that you may be healed." Galatians 6:2 says, "Carry each other's burdens, and in this way you will fulfill the law of Christ."

Our natural tendency is to avoid going to our spouse or friend in the early stages of temptation for fear of being embarrassed. However, humbling yourself and asking another to pray for you at that point is much more likely to be successful in helping you break through this bondage. (It is also a lot less embarrassing than trying in your own strength to resist the temptation and later having to confess your sin and request prayer for deliverance.) Your honest and transparent attitude may make it easier for him or her to seek your help during his or her time of temptation.

Forgiveness is not necessary when you are honest about your temptation. It is only when you deceive yourself into believing that you can overcome the temptation in your own strength and fall into it that you have to ask for forgiveness.

Ultimately, a combination of these three skills—identifying the triggering mechanisms, implementing substitute behaviors and sharing your struggle—is the "triple-pane" insulation against temptation. These skills will help you to use the Holy Spirit's "way out" to defeat the enemy's efforts to take you to the point of sinful behavior. Every time the Lord helps you to escape temptation at the point of evaluation indicated on the chart, praise Him and thank Him for keeping you from a potentially damaging or destructive behavior.[5]

QUESTIONS FOR REFLECTION

1. List several triggering events for temptation that have been particularly bothersome to you.

2. When are "addictive/sinful" cravings most prevalent?

3. Are you more susceptible to temptation when you are hungry? Angry? Lonely? Tired? Successful? Bored? Anxious? Depressed?

4. List several guards or "ways of escape" you plan to employ the next time you become aware you are being tempted. Be specific.

5. What are some legitimate and healthy ways to reward yourself when you have done well or been successful? Examples might include taking a walk, playing a sport, resting, attending a concert or reading a book.

6

IS SOMEONE WATCHING THE NEIGHBORHOOD?

"As iron sharpens iron, so one man sharpens another."
—Proverbs 27:17

Neighborhood watch programs are designed to allow local residents to assist one another in monitoring the community. No one individual is able to sense every potential threat to the neighborhood, but when a group of people keep their eyes open and are on the alert, crime rates go down and the community is a safer place to live.

This cooperative concept of keeping neighbors safe has a spiritual application. As Christians, we should be looking out for our fellow believers, just as they should be looking out for us. When applied to the area of sexual purity, it seems to work best in one-to-one partnerships. The verse from Proverbs at the beginning of this chapter is a ringing endorsement for teams of two. The book of Ecclesiastes also makes a strategic comment regarding the value of partnerships:

> Two are better than one, because they have a good return for their work: If one falls down, his friend can help him up. But pity the man who falls and has no one to help him up! Also, if two lie down together, they will keep warm. But how can one keep warm alone? Though one may be overpowered, two can defend themselves. A cord of three strands is not quickly broken. (4:9-12)

The New Testament speaks of the spiritual benefits of group interaction in such verses as Hebrews 10:24, which states, "And let us consider how we may spur *one another* on toward love and good deeds." In fact, there are more than thirty "one another" passages in the New Testament.

The frequency with which this phrase appears suggests that implementing the partnering concept into one's daily life should be an extremely significant priority for the disciple of Christ. Consider the following "one another" passages:

"A new command I give you: *Love* one another. As I have loved you, so you must love one another" (John 13:34).

"By this all men will know that you are my disciples, if you *love* one another" (John 13:35).

"Be *devoted* to one another in brotherly love. *Honor* one another above yourselves" (Romans 12:10).

"Let the word of Christ dwell in you richly as you *teach and admonish* one another with all wisdom, and as you sing psalms, hymns and spiritual songs with gratitude in your hearts to God" (Colossians 3:16).

"Therefore *encourage* one another and build each other up, just as in fact you are doing" (1 Thessalonians 5:11).

ACCOUNTABILITY PARTNERS

It is utterly crucial that men and women build systems of accountability into the fiber and fabric of their lives. The maxim "two are better than one" is also true in the sphere of sexual purity. We desperately need to incorporate accountability relationships into our lives to preserve our spiritual integrity. Dr. Howard Hendricks made this alarming assessment: "A man who is not in a group with other men is an accident waiting to happen."[1]

A study by Dallas Theological Seminary discovered that 250 pastors who fell into sexual sin had one striking constant in common: They had *no accountability partner or system.*[2] As noted in chapter 2, the number of ministers who are engaging in sexual sin is increasing every day. Pastors and parishioners both need someone to bring them to account, which simply means *to make them answer for their conduct!*

The Bible offers many examples of accountability relationships. Encounters with some of the heroes of the Holy Book spared men and nations

from catastrophic disaster. One such incident occurred after the children of Israel were delivered
from the Egyptians at the Red Sea. The human
convoy (which some scholars estimate at three
million people) was in need of advice, counsel
and judgment, and Moses foolishly tried to do it
all by himself.

The voice of reason came in the form of Jethro, Moses' father-in-law, who observed that
Moses was trying to judge all the cases of the
people, a task that was consuming him "from
morning till evening" each day (Exodus 18:13).
Jethro presented this assessment and suggestion
to the great Jewish leader:

> Moses' father-in-law replied, "What you are
> doing is not good. You and these people who
> come to you will only wear yourselves out.
> The work is too heavy for you; you cannot
> handle it alone. Listen now to me and I will
> give you some advice, and may God be with
> you. You must be the people's representative
> before God and bring their disputes to him.
> Teach them the decrees and laws, and show
> them the way to live and the duties they are
> to perform. But select capable men from all
> the people—men who fear God, trustworthy
> men who hate dishonest gain—and appoint
> them as officials over thousands, hundreds,
> fifties and tens. Have them serve as judges
> for the people at all times, but have them
> bring every difficult case to you; the simple
> cases they can decide themselves. That will

make your load lighter, because they will
share it with you. If you do this and God
so commands, you will be able to stand the
strain, and all these people will go home sat-
isfied."

Moses listened to his father-in-law and
did everything he said. He chose capable
men from all Israel and made them leaders
of the people, officials over thousands, hundreds, fifties and tens. They served as judges
for the people at all times. The difficult cases
they brought to Moses, but the simple ones
they decided themselves. (Exodus 18:17–26)

Jethro's advice saved Moses from a physical
and emotional collapse. The subsequent reorga-
nizing of the nation into clusters that would be
more manageable and effective enabled this huge
conglomerate of people to be effectively coun-
seled under less-than-desirable living conditions.
Apparently, Moses had not been able to see the
inevitable consequences of continuing this im-
possible management structure. But fortunately,
Moses listened to his father-in-law, and both he
and the nation benefited from this bold, innova-
tive and necessary change!

This one-to-one interaction and transparent
relationship is featured throughout Scripture between such notable pairs as Abraham and Lot,
Elijah and Elisha and especially Paul and his apprentice, Timothy.

I (Arnold) have an accountability partner with
whom I meet on a regular basis. (I specifically

chose someone who does *not* attend the church I serve as pastor.) We regularly gather at breakfast to pray, ask each other questions and openly share what is going on in our lives. My accountability partner has requested that I ask two specific questions each time we meet:

1. "What have you looked at since the last time we met?"

2. "What is happening in your devotional life?"

These two questions turn up many issues that can prevent my Christian brother from engaging in activities that are displeasing to God and destructive to him and his family. Because an agreement has been executed prior to our sessions, my partner is fully aware that the questions are coming to him at every accountability meeting. Therefore, he has an incentive to live with his heart and mind "set on things above" (Colossians 3:1–2).

In turn, my friend asks me questions that pertain to my family, my ministry and my relationship with the Lord. He has kept me from frustration, from making a serious ministry error and has kept me far more balanced than I would ever be on my own. To be perfectly honest, both of us regret at times the answers we must give in response to the questions, but we have no regrets regarding the value of this exercise! It has helped us both cultivate a more fully devoted and disciplined life for Jesus Christ.

Accountability Models

There are many accountability models that include a list of helpful questions that two or more individuals could ask each other in a small-group setting. EMERGE Ministries, the successful counseling center in Akron, Ohio, provides a sample template of questions that could be inserted into a regular accountability relationship to help its participants guard against sexual indiscretions and general moral missteps. These eight questions are as follows:

1. Have you been with anyone, anywhere, that could appear compromising?
2. Have you entertained any inappropriate fantasies in your thought life?
3. Have you viewed or read any sexually explicit material?
4. Have any of your financial dealings lacked integrity?
5. Have you spent adequate time in Bible study and prayer?
6. Have you given priority time to your family?
7. Have you been faithful in your work for the Lord?
8. **HAVE YOU JUST LIED TO ME?**[3]

Networking is a necessary component of any healthy model of Christian discipleship. As Scripture says, two are better than one, and the apprentice of Jesus Christ who tries to go it alone is often blindsided and certainly more vulnerable to temptation than the disciple who links up with others in the journey of faith.

In the game of baseball, the first-base and third-base coaches play a subtle but significant role. They provide the players with added perspective and viewpoints. Their counsel often saves the base runner from a drastic error of judgment; their encouragement often enhances the runner's chances of getting to the next base or scoring the winning run. In the same way, accountability partners and groups provide us an advantage we can never have when we run the race alone.

In *Blue Like Jazz*, Donald Miller shares a conversation with his friend on the necessity of cops. The author's final words resonate with the power of accountability: "Sometimes I think, you know, if there were not cops, I would be fine, and I probably would. I was taught right from wrong when I was a kid. But the truth is, I drive completely different when there is a cop behind me than when there isn't."[4]

I am concluding this chapter with a statement by a college student who attended a church under my ministry. Just prior to graduating from Syracuse University, he wrote a powerful testimony on accountability relationships in his collegiate life:

> For me, accountability has been a huge part
> of my life, not only in college, but since I
> was a part of the youth group at Trinity a

few years ago. When I left for college, I was strongly encouraged, and actively searched for both a group and a single person I could be accountable with. The accountability of the LifeGroup that I was a part of, and now lead, was not as deep as the one-on-one discipleship I was a part of. In the LifeGroups, we would mainly be accountable to each other in regards to devotional times, prayer life, and relationship issues we as college men face. We figured the group we had, about eight or so, was a little too big to go very deep. However, we decided that one-on-one was needed as a surplus to the group.

I started my one-on-one discipleship my second semester, freshman year. The guy I met with was a couple years older than me, and we shared similar sports interests, which is what first brought us together. Each week we would grab something to eat and go through a chunk of Scripture, on average a chapter a week. At first, that was all it was, meal and Bible study. But soon it became a safe place where we could each explain what we were going through. Many of the times it was the same as the LifeGroup, though we did talk about pornography a few times. But I realized that even though we didn't talk about our pornography problems every time we talked, we both knew that we could talk if we had gone to a Web site, etc., that week. One thing we talked about for a couple weeks when we both dealt with pornography issues was setting up a program where we

would be sent every Web site we visited automatically. Knowing that that was a possibility
set me on the right path almost immediately.

Even though my one-on-one partner has
graduated, the impact of that one relationship changed my life very quickly. And even
though we didn't always bring up certain
issues right away, we both knew when there
was a problem. I think the best thing about
it, too, was the fact that even though he was
a few years older than me, we were accountable to each other. It also helped to know that
I wasn't the only one going through what I
was going through. That, I think, is one of the
biggest things Christians go through—the
thought that "I am the only one doing this, so
I need to hide it and keep it to myself."

Now that I am coleading a LifeGroup,
we have made it an important aspect of
the group to talk about what we are going
through, most of the time in a lot of detail.
As I graduate, I know I will deeply miss the
connections I have made with the guys in
my group, and I am making it an important
priority to find a group like this, as well as a
one-on-one opportunity wherever I end up.
It has become an important part of my life,
and I hope to have more of these groups and
people throughout my life.[5]

QUESTIONS FOR REFLECTION

1. Can you think of a situation where counsel from a family member or friend spared you great embarrassment or failure?

2. Do you have an accountability partner? How often do you meet, and where do you meet?

3. What are the two most important questions that you would advise an accountability partner to ask you each time you meet?

7

Fixing Broken Windows

*It is critical that we repair the brokenness that is the
by-product of sexual transgression.*

*"Brothers, if someone is caught in a sin, you who are
spiritual should restore him gently. But watch yourself, or you also may be tempted."*
—Galatians 6:1

How much pain are you in right now as a result
of your sexual choices? You may have come
to this chapter aware that you have allowed a
number of broken windows to fester in your soul.
Untended broken windows have left the neighborhood of your heart a spiritual ghetto. Porn or
other sexual transgressions have resulted in anger, guilt, sadness, blame, low self-esteem and/or
hopelessness. Perhaps you have lost the trust of
a spouse, the respect of your children or the con-

fidence of your friends. Maybe you've even lost your position or job as a result of inappropriate sexual behaviors. What you thought was in your control now has a stranglehold over you.

The biggest barrier we experience at EMERGE Ministries is trying to assess the amount of pain a client is in when seeking treatment. As EMERGE's founder, Dr. Richard Dobbins, was fond of saying, "Until the pain of remaining the same is greater than the pain of change . . . people tend to stay the same. It is when the pain of remaining the same becomes so great that one cannot stay the same . . . this is when change can occur." How much pain are you in?

How can I rebuild my broken world?

Perhaps you have come to the end of yourself and you are finally ready to cry out to God. Good! This is the true beginning of a journey to "fix the broken windows" of the soul. The goal of this chapter is to offer some practical advice on how to repair the brokenness that is the by-product of sexual transgression.

First, fixing broken windows requires a new mind-set. You will need to prepare emotionally for a long period of recovery, along with enhanced vigilance and consistency. Even after months of relative victory, you must remind yourself that you will always be vulnerable in this area of your life, so you can never relax your guard against temptation.

Our experience indicates that recovering from an addiction to pornography is similar to recovering from any other physical or emotional addiction. You must understand that addictive disorders are both spiritual as well as psychological in nature. While your will is a necessary dynamic in recovery, *it is not sufficient*. You must realize your need for the power of eternal life, which can only be found in the person of Jesus Christ (see John 8:36). This is not a "quick fix" or an easy process. You will not break free from this kind of bondage without a struggle. The enemy won't let go easily, either. In addition, you will need to find another person who will support you in this battle.

ROLE OF THE SPOUSE

Although the focus of treatment will typically be on you, your spouse must also be involved as well. After all, your involvement in pornography has seriously affected your sex life. Your spouse shouldn't be surprised to find that the intimate relationship you share has been fractured by the sexual fantasies you have been living out through the use of porn. As part of your recovery, you must address your own vulnerability, intimacy and bonding needs with your spouse.

SOME QUESTIONS TO ANSWER HONESTLY AT THIS POINT

You must realize that your goal in recovery is far more than just "sin management." God is interested in a complete renovation of your heart and character. This is like replacing the glass in a broken window rather than just putting tape over the holes. We will address the specifics of godly character formation in chapter 8.

The first and most important question you need to answer is, *Are you committed to your recovery?* Do you understand that this is a moment-by-moment, hour-by-hour, day-by-day battle? Are you amenable to accountability? Are you willing to be transparent and honest? Or are you merely interested in saving your marriage, your reputation, your family or your job?

Barriers in the initial phase of treatment often include such things as denial, pride, a desire to please those in authority and fear of having another failure.

FROM BROKEN WINDOWS TO BROKEN HEARTS: CONFESSION AND HONESTY

Begin the recovery and healing process by confessing to God that you need His mercy to cleanse and purify you. Read Psalm 51:2, 7, 8, 10, 17; 2 Timothy 3; 2 Peter 2; and James 5:16. Throw yourself on God's mercy.

Make no attempt to justify, minimize or blame others for your choices. Spend an extensive time in prayer (and also, perhaps, fasting). Talk to God honestly about the details of your sin. Ask the Holy Spirit to convict you of any selfish attitude, hidden resentment, arrogance or pride that obstructs His work in your life. Remember the words of Psalm 51:17: "A broken and contrite heart, O God, you will not despise." Deep repentance brings profound and lasting change.

Allow the Holy Spirit to have access to the broken windows of your heart. Allow Him to clarify the exact nature of your bondage to sexual sin.

A MODIFIED "TWELVE-STEP" PROGRAM

Based upon the original Alcoholics Anonymous Twelve-Step Program, we have found that systematically completing the following steps of humility and surrender are required for victory:

> 1. I admitted I was powerless over pornography (and/or other sexual perversion—name it specifically) and that my life had become unmanageable.
> 2. I came to believe that Jesus Christ could restore me to sanity.
> 3. I made a decision to turn my will and my life over to the care of Jesus Christ.
> 4. I made a searching and fearless moral inventory of myself.
> 5. I admitted to God, to myself and to another human being the exact nature of my wrongs.
> 6. I was entirely ready to have God remove all these defects of my character.
> 7. I humbly asked Him to remove all my shortcomings.
> 8. I made a list of all persons I had harmed and became willing to make amends to them all.
> 9. I made direct amends to people wherever possible, except when to do it would injure them or others.
> 10. I continued to take a personal inven-

tory and, when I was wrong, promptly admitted it.

11. I sought through prayer and meditation to improve my conscious contact with God through Jesus Christ, praying only for knowledge of His will for me and the power to carry it out.

12. Having had a spiritual awakening as a result of these steps, I tried to carry this message to others who struggle with pornography (or other sexual sins) and to practice these principles in my life.

Reread chapters 5 and 6 of this book. Pay particular attention to the "Old Self/New Self Model" and the necessity of having someone "help you watch the neighborhood of your heart." This accountability partner needs to be a close confidant who has the authority and your full consent to confront and challenge you. Ask the Holy Spirit to suggest the name of someone who would be willing to mentor you on your journey to recovery.

A LONG OBEDIENCE IN THE SAME DIRECTION

Eugene Peterson's book on the Psalms, *A Long Obedience in the Same Direction*, sets the tone of the life before you. That title is a quote from Friedrich Nietzsche, who wrote, "The essential thing 'in heaven and earth' is . . . that there should be long obedience in the same direction; there thereby results, and has always resulted in the long run, something which has made life worth living."[1]

The concept of "a long obedience in the same direction" is what the Bible calls *steadfastness*, *faithfulness* and *perseverance*. It is a marathon, not just a sprint. It means to get on the road and stay the course, however difficult. Hang in there. Stay with the program. Be patient and trust the process as well as your heavenly Healer.

WHAT CHANGES CAN I EXPECT?

You will begin to notice that you have become attuned to the inner promptings of the Holy Spirit. You will notice that you are beginning to exercise a different attitude toward your spouse, considering his or her needs above your own. You will also notice a change in your devotional life. Whereas time with God may have been perfunctory, superficial or nonexistent before, you will now look forward to the personal one-to-one contact with the Lord Jesus Christ as you talk with Him about your day and the things you are doing together.

As time goes on, you will begin to notice a change in your attraction to the allurements of the world (sports, newspapers, Internet, TV, secular talk shows). Others may begin to comment on the softness in your countenance, on your renewed passion for God and love for others.

NOT OUT OF THE WOODS

As you begin to make a recovery from the stranglehold of sexual addiction, don't assume that the enemy is going to slip away quietly. You will still be vulnerable to temptations. Remember, the enemy builds strongholds in secrecy and enforces them by silence. Break the silence and you will break the stronghold. The enemy always takes us further than we intended to go, keeps us longer than we intended to stay, and the price is greater than we ever intended to pay. He seeks to blind us from the devastating consequences of sin.

On the other hand, you must appropriate the truth of God's Word, where He promises that, "If we confess our sins, he is faithful and just and will forgive us our sins and purify us from all unrighteousness" (1 John 1:9). In other words, God is willing to forgive us of any sin that we are willing to confess to Him. What marvelous grace!

Fixing the Broken Windows

As you continue on this personal journey of hope and recovery, realize that you are not alone. God is with you. He loves you. He has not abandoned you. You may be reading this chapter at what you perceive to be a very low point in your life. There is hope and help for you. Bring your broken windows to Jesus. He is the master craftsman and sincerely desires to build within you a new heart. Remember, God wants a broken spirit and heart. He won't despise these realities.

QUESTIONS FOR REFLECTION

1. Does your church have a Celebrate Recovery group? If not, find one in your area and consider joining it. Even if you are not involved in a Celebrate Recovery program, are you willing to work through the "Twelve Steps" with a close confidant?

2. What losses have you experienced as you have given yourself over to sexual impurity?

3. How do you know from personal experience that willpower alone hasn't worked?

4. How have you been denying, minimizing or justifying your sinful sexual behavior?

5. Who will be your accountability partner? Who will you consider to be a mentor for you in your process of recovery?

6. Did you read the passages noted on p. 92 on forgiveness and restoration? Journal your responses to these verses.

8

ARMING THE ALARM SYSTEM

*If thou intendest heartily to serve God, and avoid sin
in any one instance, refuse not the hardest and most
severe advice that is prescribed in order to it, though
possibly it be a stranger to thee; for whatsoever it be,
custom will make it easy.*[1]
—Jeremy Taylor

*"Do not merely listen to the word, and so deceive
yourselves. Do what it says."*
—James 1:22

Today, many safety-conscious homeowners
have installed alarm systems in their homes to
alert them if intruders break in. Though they can
be expensive and require some time to learn how
to use them, they are well worth the trouble if they
help keep the family and their property secure.

Similarly, it is also worthwhile to install alarm

systems in our minds and souls, to warn us of impending danger and moral failure. The number of possible intruders—some human, some technological—that seek to undermine our dignity, profit from our promiscuity and destroy our character and families has proliferated in recent years. If we can be warned ahead of time that a dangerous stimulus is seeking to engage our attention, we can be prepared to respond with the right attitudes and actions, and avoid the consequences of choosing the *wrong* reaction.

How can we actively "guard our hearts" and "set our minds on things above"? How do we arm the alarm system so that we can escape the despair, guilt and judgment that accompany a sexual sin? One of the most effective ways to do this is through a *spiritual exercise program*—one that develops the type of character that resonates with the life of Christ, acquires the mind of Christ, develops the habits of Christ and responds as Christ did to temptation. In this chapter we want to place before you a practical plan for a spiritual exercise program that you can actually begin to implement today.

BEYOND MERE "SIN MANAGEMENT"

You can wash a broken window, but it does no good if it leaves the window broken. We are not talking about a superficial religiosity. Our focus must now move beyond merely a shallow and ineffectual cycle of "sin management" to the point of *deep spiritual formation*. How are the mind and heart of Christ sincerely and ultimately formed in us? The answer to that begins with a second question, which you need to consider very carefully:

Wouldn't it be an amazing work of the Holy Spirit as well as a profound change in our character to get to the point where we would, with a perfectly clear conscience, view just as much porn as we want?

You may be thinking, *What?! Did I read that last question correctly?* Yes, you did, and there is a precise purpose and spiritual depth behind that question. Jesus wants to be formed in us to the point that we will do whatever we want—and, it will be *the exact same thing He would do.* So if Jesus is formed in us to the point that our desires become the same as His desires, the question becomes, *how much porn would Jesus indulge in?* How did Jesus confront the temptations that came to Him—temptations that were just the same as the ones we face (see Hebrews 4:15)?

Refer back to the first and second chapters of this book. Who is the owner (landlord) of my body now that I am joined to Christ? *He is.* So, in your honest appraisal, do you consistently honor Christ in your body? Remember, your body is as much God's gift to you as is your soul and spirit. You are a mere steward over it, important as a caretaker but ultimately accountable to the "Landlord." If you allow broken windows of the

soul to go unrepaired, there are serious consequences.

Dr. Richard Dobbins is fond of saying, "We
have no shortage of 'ought-tos' in the Scripture
and in our pulpits; we often have a shortage of
'how-tos.'" It's time to take a serious crash course
in the "how-tos" of safeguarding our hearts and
minds from persistent and potent temptations.

THE "HOW-TOS" FOR THE BIBLICAL "OUGHT-TOS"

Do you believe it is possible to do what Jesus
says to do? Is it possible to enter into a training
regimen that would produce the type of character that would enable you to habitually respond
to temptation the way that Jesus did?

What sort of training should you engage in
to achieve this goal? As Dallas Willard notes in
his book *Divine Conspiracy*, "When you teach children or adults to ride a bicycle or swim, they actually do ride bikes or swim on appropriate occa-
sions. You don't just teach them that they *ought* to
ride bicycles, or that it is *good* to ride bicycles, or
that they should be ashamed if they don't."[2]

We need much more than simple behavior
modification, although modified behavior is certainly a valuable first step in dealing with sexual
sin and other broken windows of the soul. In
previous chapters of this book, we have outlined
the real problem and provided some initial comments on "putting off the old self and putting on
the new self." The chief problem is that unless

there is a deeper change, *a change in our character*, we are simply managing the sin problem and not being transformed into the type of person who would easily and naturally do the things Jesus would do if He were us.

We can quote alarming statistics, deplore the encroaching problem of pornography and even cite numerous reasons and quote Scripture verses as to why one should avoid even the appearance of evil. But the question remains: How can I live my life in a different dimension that regularly appropriates the abundant life promised to me in Christ, with subsequent spiritual fruit (see Galatians 5:22–26)? As mentioned previously, the will is *necessary but inadequate* to develop the life texture of Christ.

Outward conformity, religious traditions, and even correct doctrines are vital to stifling the vicious cycle of temptation, of course, but, as Willard notes, "They do not produce transformation of the inner self."[3]

One of the primary objectives of the practical "how-tos" for curbing temptation is to fall deeply in love with God. We urge you in the strongest terms to fill your mind with the love of God. Also, you must systematically work to replace the embodied habits ("enslavement"—see John 8:34 and Romans 6:6) that have dominated you up to this point in your struggle with sexual sins. The body is the place where ingrained habits manifest themselves. Many of us have indeed become so accustomed to the "broken windows" of our lives that we may assume there is nothing that can be done to remedy our brokenness—that we are forever slaves to our old habit patterns.

First Things First

It is crucial, first and foremost, that you begin to actually express your love to God with all of your heart, soul, mind and strength. Realize that *God isn't mad at you*. He loves you deeply. He sincerely desires a complete and honest relationship with you. He wants you to know that you are not only loveable, but also valuable, forgivable and *changeable*. It may be helpful to purchase a cross or some other emblem whose purpose it is to remind you of God and in so doing help to keep the Lord Jesus ever in the forefront your mind. Take a few moments to read Romans 8:31–39 in several different translations and meditate on the truth that God is really *for* you, not *against* you!

If you don't fall deeply in love with Christ, you place yourself at great risk to believe that you are left to your own devices to fix the broken windows of your soul. And yet, nothing could be further from the truth. God *really does* desire good for you. Love Him and continue to fall in love with Him.

Second, recognize that God does not leave you helpless under the power of evil. Because of your personal history, previous practices, past failures and habits, you may believe your personal situation to be hopeless. *You must not believe this lie!* Habits are simply that—habits. They have been formed over time by practice and have become largely automatic.

When you first learned to drive a car, you were totally conscious of each action you took before you left the driveway—everything from seat position to adjusting the mirrors to buckling the seat belt. Now, however, through constant, repetitive practice, you perform activities largely unconsciously, in some cases "multitasking" to the point of doing everything necessary to drive, while simultaneously talking on your cell phone or checking a map. The process by which we learn to habitually indulge in—or avoid—sexual sins works in a surprisingly similar manner.

Some "broken windows" of your private life have been broken so long that you have come to believe that they cannot be fixed. Perhaps you have gotten to the point mentioned in the last chapter—one of utter despair and heartfelt repentance. Good! This is an essential first step in the healing process. Those windows still remain broken, however, and unless they are swiftly repaired, it will only be a matter of time until you are overtaken by temptation again. As Dallas Willard makes abundantly clear, "Our bodies do what they know to do."[4]

Your habits, or "windows of the soul," can—and must—be changed, repaired and replaced. The good news is that you are not on your own, nor *can* you be, to make these changes. Yes, you are involved in the healing process (as we will discuss later), but it is an interaction of your intention and choices with the power and inner working of the Holy Spirit. Philippians 2:12–13 puts it this way: "Work out your salvation with fear and trembling, for it is God who works in you to will and to act according to his good purpose." While we are at work to develop what God intends for us, He is also at work in us to bring to fruition in our daily lives the life of Jesus Christ (see 2 Corinthians 3:18).

THE ROLE OF THE SPIRITUAL DISCIPLINES

We thank God for every Christian writer who has helped men and women to manage their sexual desires and receive forgiveness for sexual sin. We trust that you will install filtering software in your computer, establish an accountability partner and observe other practices that we have already mentioned. But we must not be content to stop there. To really address the root problem of our broken windows, we must go deeper still, into spiritual territory.

At this point in the book, we hope you are truly motivated to enter into this new order of life, confident in the wisdom of Jesus Christ and willing to listen to and follow His teachings. To help you enter in, we want to introduce you to a series of *disciplines*—structured practices—for advancing in the spiritual life. It should come as no surprise that there are spiritual disciplines for the Christian life. Any worthwhile endeavor, such as sports, music or writing, has its own set of disciplines for success. As Donald Whitney notes, "The freedom to grow in godliness—to naturally express Christ's character through your own personality—is in large part dependent on a deliberate cultivation of the spiritual disciplines."[5]

By definition, a discipline is something that is within our power to do and which allows us (over time) to be able to do what we could not do otherwise. Having completed a number of marathons, for instance, I (Don) would never be so foolish as to show up on the day of the event without having completed many weeks of training. A training program for a marathon always begins small and gradually builds up the runner's endurance, so that on the day of the race, he or she can do what needs to be done to make it across the finish line.

THE PURPOSE OF THE SPIRITUAL DISCIPLINES IS NOT THE SPIRITUAL DISCIPLINES

Just as training for a marathon is not the purpose of a marathon, neither are spiritual disciplines an end unto themselves. Rather, they are a *means* to an end. The training in godliness that the Apostle Paul wrote about (see 1 Timothy 4:7) was not to glorify the training; rather it was a means to an end (godliness). Spiritual disciplines enable us to receive more of Jesus' life and power.[6] Rather than becoming cold legalisms, the spiritual disciplines develop a love relationship with Jesus and produce a changed character—and by extension, a different lifestyle. The Apostle Paul's prescription for Christlikeness is described by Willard in *The Spirit of the Disciplines.*

> We can become like Christ in character and in power and thus realize our highest ideals of well-being and well-doing. . . . My central claim is that we *can* become like Christ by doing one thing—by following him in the overall style of life he chose for himself. If we have faith in Christ, we must believe that he knew how to live. We can, through faith and grace, become like Christ by practicing the types of activities he engaged in, by arranging our whole lives around the types of activities he himself practiced in order to remain constantly at home in the fellowship of his Father. . . . Such things as solitude and silence, prayer, simple and sacrificial living, intense study and meditation upon God's Word and God's ways, and service to others.[7]

GETTING STARTED

The late Donald Grey Barnhouse once preached a sermon entitled, "The Life of Supreme Triumph in Christ." He opens the message by quoting several lines from a children's poem: "For the want of a nail the shoe was lost / For the want of a shoe the horse was lost / For the want of a horse the rider was lost / For the want of a rider the battle was lost . . . all for the want of a horseshoe nail." Consistent with our "Broken Windows" theory, this poem illustrates how small things can become big problems if not addressed quickly.

On the other hand, as Malcolm Gladwell points out in *The Tipping Point*, small, positive changes in the way we behave can introduce a new rhythm to life, allowing a man or woman to reach a "tipping point" where life begins to move along in a new and profoundly healthier direction.[8]

To kick-start this transformative process, begin today and each day by reflecting on the person of Jesus Christ. Talk to Him; listen to Him; let Him know that today you will intentionally look for Him. Second, ask Jesus for His help in becoming His *disciple*—His apprentice in the craft of life. Third, let Jesus know that you intend to trust and obey Him today.

One way to arm the alarm system of your heart is to study the Word of God. Psalm 119 provides the most intense study of God's Word in the Bible. The passage poses a highly significant question and then provides some powerful counsel: "How can a young man keep his way pure? By living according to your word" (119:9). This Word—the Bible—functions like a light to our path (119:105). If we do not process the Word of God regularly, the batteries of our spiritual flashlights start to dim, and eventually we are stumbling and falling as we journey through life in the dark.

But if the disciple of Christ is a student of the Word, then when the trap is set and an opportunity is presented to commit sexual sin, he will default to his familiar knowledge of the Scriptures, rather than to old habits. Jesus Himself, when He faced the temptations of Satan, not only recalled the Word in His mind, He *spoke* it to the devil in His defense (see Matthew 4:1–11; Luke 4:1–13). So, one way to arm the system is to meditate and make incarnate the revelation of God. Although it sounds old-fashioned, some old remedies are still the most effective!

Furthermore, look into God's Word (especially the Gospels of Jesus' life) and discover what it is that He commands. Remember, Jesus said, "If you love me, you will obey what I command" (John 14:15). As you begin to obey Christ with confident love, you will find your mind and heart abiding more and more in the attitudes and spiritual strength of Christ. Take note, then, of how your spiritual "muscles" begin to develop and observe how spiritual fruit—love, kindness, self-control—is produced in your life as outward evidence of the inward reality that your heart is undergoing a transformation (see Galatians 5:22–23).

Keep the love of Jesus always before you. Keep abiding in Him. Don't try to "bear fruit" of healthy attitudes and pure behaviors on your own; instead stay present with Jesus throughout your day and learn to rely on Him for the courage and resolution to avoid and overcome temptation. Abide in Him (see John 8:31–32; 15:5). Finally, as you begin to experience victory over sexual (and other) temptations, use the power that is being formed in your life for the good of others.

Share what you are learning about living in the kingdom with another person.

The spiritual disciplines established in Scripture and Christian tradition are many and varied. Here is just a sampling: fasting and prayer, study and service, submission and solitude, confession and worship, meditation and silence, simplicity, frugality, sacrifice and celebration. As noted previously, a spiritual discipline is an activity that is in our power to do, which, by God's mysterious and surprising intervention, enables us to do something we cannot do by our *direct effort*.

SETTING THE ALARM SYSTEM

Never forget that the eyes are "the windows of the soul" and that sight is often the entry point at which sexual sin is given incubation, prior to a person's actual indulgence in that behavior. The story of Potiphar's wife inviting Joseph to be physically intimate with her includes the telling detail that "Joseph was well-built and handsome" and "after a while his master's wife *took notice* of" him (Genesis 39:6-7). Likewise, the preface to Samson's night with a prostitute includes a reference to a dangerous visual stimulus: "Samson went to Gaza, where he *saw* a prostitute" (Judges 16:1). In fact, the most infamous sexual scenario recorded in Scripture begins with King David's illicit attraction to Bathsheba.

> In the spring, at the time when kings go off to war, David sent Joab out with the king's

men and the whole Israelite army. They de-
stroyed the Ammonites and besieged Rabbah.
But David remained in Jerusalem. One evening David got up from his bed and walked
around on the roof of the palace. From the
roof he *saw* a woman bathing. The woman
was very beautiful. (2 Samuel 11:1–2)

David was arrested by Bathsheba's beauty
and his prolonged look at her naked body veered
him onto a destructive pathway, one that ultimately resulted in the death of a man and of an
infant—and the withdrawal of God's full blessing
upon his kingship and his people. The devastation of a heroic man's life began with the retinas
of his eyes reflecting a stunning physical speci-
men who was not his wife.

In the same way, if we find ourselves taking
a prolonged look that could lead to a prolonged
and sinful plan, to others being hurt, and to an
elaborate cover-up of our actions, we can be sure
we have looked too long. We must keep a vigilant
watch over our eyes to avoid viewing the naked-
ness of anyone who is not our spouse, or we risk
disastrous consequences to our marriages, families and ministries.

One specific modern tool to prevent the failures that start with a sight trigger is Internet filtering software. The purpose of these programs
is to prevent pornographic pictures from appear-
ing on a computer screen. Many of these software
packages are reasonably priced and equipped

with various filtering features. Net Nanny, Safe Eyes, CYBERsitter, CyberPatrol, MaxProtect, FilterPak, Netmop and Norton Parental Controls are all affordable and highly effective filtering software. If you have any doubt that you really need such software, remember the stories of Potiphar's wife and Samson's tryst with a prostitute—both sprang from the allure of a seductive visual stimulus that dragged their eyes, and by extension their minds, into the close orbit of iniquity.

A JOURNAL OF CONSEQUENCES

Another technique to short-circuit recurrent temptations is to journal out the consequences of a sexual sin. Name specifically the people who would be hurt by your actions; write down the things you would lose if your sin were to be made public. It is paramount to your success over sin that you grasp just how massive the collateral damage of sexual missteps would be—and how it would affect not only you, but your spouse, children, grandchildren, friends, neighbors, colleagues at work and even fellow church members.

Most sexual sins are secret, committed in darkness, but the effects are often revealed in the light. It is foolish to pretend that there is no pleasure in sin for a short time—even Scripture does not deny that fact (see Hebrews 11:25). In our battle against formidable and enthralling temptations, we do ourselves a disservice if we fail to acknowledge the reality of a secret sin's momentary pleasure or its disastrous long-term consequences.

John Piper, in a sermon entitled "Sexual Failure and God's Mission," wrote this chilling and pulsating warning:

> The great tragedy is not masturbation or fornication or pornography. The tragedy is that Satan uses the guilt of these failures to strip you of every radical dream you ever had, or might have. In their place, he gives you a happy, safe, secure, American life of superficial pleasures until you die in your lakeside rocking chair.[9]

Another warning to consider is that famous biblical maxim, "Pride goes before destruction, a haughty spirit before a fall" (Proverbs 16:18). Anyone who aspires to live a moral life and pursue ethical excellence cannot afford to become overconfident in early successes over temptation. Life is full of twists and turns, changeable weather, unanticipated ups and downs—all of which throw us off our spiritual routine and often cause us to let down our guard.

C.J. Mahaney and Robin Boisvert put this issue into perspective by reminding us that "we *have been* delivered from the *penalty* of sin; we *are being* delivered from the *power* of sin; we *shall be* delivered from the *presence* of sin."[10] In other words, though we are freed from the penalty of our failures, there is still a power struggle—a *war*, if you will—between our flesh and spirit, between what we know we should do and what we are tempted to do in opposition to that "should." All sports fans have witnessed athletic teams scoring early and often and presuming their game was won, only to let down their guard, lose their momentum and find themselves lying in the dust of defeat by the end of the game to a more tenacious opponent. When we reach the moment where we believe we cannot fall, we are likely closest to the jagged edges of a steep cliff!

Finally, keep in mind that you cannot fix the broken windows of your soul solely by your own efforts. You do have a role in the process, however; you are involved in this special labor of purity by choice. Remember, the purpose of the spiritual disciplines is to place us before God. For example, when you fast a meal in order to focus on God, you bring yourself into the presence of God, who will do for (and through) you what you cannot do for yourself. Over time, inner spiritual transformation creates in us a new heart, a new mind, a transformation of our very character. Far from a righteousness attained by our effort or "works," this transformation consists of a God-inspired, God-empowered renovation. You will be changed from a man or woman ensnared in unhealthy, discouraging habits into the kind of person who automatically does what needs to be done when it needs to be done. You can arm the alarm system of your soul by exercising the spiritual disciplines. It is a joint effort of your choices and God's astonishing, capable and inexhaustible power.

This is true freedom.[11]

Questions for Reflection

1. What can you do today to fall more deeply in love with Jesus? Would a walk outdoors help? Would listening to and singing a praise song help?

2. As you read such books as Foster's *Celebration of Discipline* and Whitney's *Spiritual Disciplines for the Christian Life* and actually practice the disciplines mentioned there, how has God met you? What do you notice happening in the habit structure of your life?

3. How do you respond to the "training" program outlined in this chapter?

4. Talk to the Lord Jesus about the following spiritual disciplines: meditation, prayer, fasting, study, simplicity, solitude, submission, service, confession, worship, guidance and celebration. Which of these would He want you to begin practicing?

5. As you do practice some of these disciplines, what are you noticing about drawing closer to the heart of Jesus? How is this relationship affecting your previously ingrained habit of sexual sin?

Two Case Studies
from the Counseling Practice of Dr. Donald Lichi

The two case studies below are typical of the stories I hear from my clients. Some of the personally revealing details have been changed, but the essence is based on actual case studies. Questions for reflection are at the end of each story.

Jerry's Story

I sometimes receive messages on my voice mail like this: "Dr. Lichi, you don't know me; I got your name from a friend [or "I heard you speak," or "I read something you wrote"] and I'm in big trouble. Will you call me right away?"

Jerry made such a call. He spoke over the phone in a sheepish, stammering, shame-filled manner. During the first session I simply asked him to tell me his story. As was typical, Jerry was first exposed to pornography at the age of eleven when he discovered a "stash of magazines" at his uncle's house. That first impression moved instantly into his long-term (permanent) memory and, despite the shame and guilt, he found himself masturbating to the images numerous times during his preteen and teenage years.

His adolescence coincided with the advent of the Internet. Jerry found that pornography was instantly available and supposedly anonymous. Depression, self-punishment, low self-esteem and promises to "never do this again" became his personal cycle of defeat and despair.

Two years ago his wife inadvertently looked at the history on the computer and discovered Jerry's hidden life. Following the confrontation, Jerry installed an "Internet screening program" on his computer and began to meet with two other men from his church for mutual accountability. They even asked the "accountability questions" listed in this book. After a couple of months of relative freedom, however, Jerry slid back into his secret life.

Sound familiar? At some point Jerry's acting out with Internet pornography was discovered on his work computer and he was fired. This is when he made the crisis call to my office. The scenario could have been much different if he had recognized the long history of seemingly small compromises (broken windows) that were left unattended.

During our counseling sessions I asked Jerry to be open and honest and tell me his story. I share it with his permission as an illustration of what this book is all about. Of course a few of the personally identifying details are adjusted but in fact, this is his story.

Some things are critical to note as we unfold the story of Jerry's life. Note for example that his first exposure to porn was when he was just age eleven. This is common in our hyper-sexualized culture.

Jerry described times as a teen when he would arrange his schedule so that he could be alone on the family computer. When he was in college, he often made excuses to avoid social functions with his roommates in order to have some time alone on the computer to view pornography. He found himself going through the typical addictive cycle. He became preoccupied and engrossed with thoughts of sex and found himself obsessively searching for sexual stimulation. The preoccupation gave way to ritualization leading to routines that led up to acting out. For Jerry, this meant getting up earlier, staying up later and looking forward to times when his roommates would be out doing other activities.

Later, when he was married, Jerry anticipated times when his wife was out of the house, allowing him a couple of hours to indulge. Next came compulsiveness—the actual act of viewing the porn and masturbating to the images. At this point he felt totally out of control, and in despair he made numerous promises to himself to "never act out again." But the cycle repeated itself with increasing frequency, risk taking and activity.

Jerry admitted that not only did he try to hide his behavior, he often would go for several weeks and have "victory." After all, this was a personal and private matter that he could manage on his own. However, he noticed that when he was stressed (or hungry, angry, lonely, tired, bored, anxious or depressed) he found himself returning to his "safe place"—Internet porn. Without getting help, Jerry was on a path of increased risk-taking behavior that eventually led him to sexually related chat rooms, sexual humor and innuendo with others while online and lunchtime trips to local strip clubs.

I commended Jerry for finally having the courage to seek professional help. In his case he was given the ultimatum: Get counseling or lose the marriage. I quickly informed him that while it was critical for his "will" to be involved in the healing process, it was inadequate for the job. After all, hadn't he unsuccessfully tried the "willpower" thing for years? I reminded Jerry that his will was necessary but insufficient. But when his will showed up and he was prepared to be totally honest with God, the Holy Spirit would indeed show up in mighty power on his behalf. We traced his personal and sexual history and identified the first exposure to porn along with the "small" compromises he made over the years.

Through a great deal of pain, joint sessions with his wife, the practice of the spiritual disciplines, a tough-minded men's support group, open communication, honesty and utter dependence on God, Jerry has made significant gains in his personal and family life. He continues to work through the "steps to recovery" and continues to practice the skills of the Old Self/New Self model. Jerry's marriage is thriving, and his family is restored. God is using him to help lead a Celebrate Recovery group in his church. But when I think of the pain that his wife endured, the loss of his job, the alienation from his children for more than a year, the loss of self-respect and the pain of recovery, Jerry would be the first to say, "Fix the broken windows early on!"

Is he still tempted? Of course! We are still living in a world that constantly seeks to entice and lure us away from authentic intimacy. But Jerry is wise enough now to recognize (at least most of the time) what situations and circumstances are risky for him, and he has a plan in place to deal with temptation when it is still a thought, fantasy or idea.

He also continues to build safeguards in his life. He knows there are certain places he needs to avoid, certain shows he cannot watch and certain types of conversations and jesting in which he cannot engage.

Is Jerry's story unique? Unfortunately not. Perhaps you can identify with aspects of his life. From what you've learned in this book, reflect on the following questions:

1. What were some of the "broken windows" Jerry failed to address early in his life experience?

2. Trace the path toward addiction (review the stages of addiction discussed in chapter 4). Can you identify the stages Jerry went through on his own path to addiction?

3. What were some of the first steps as well as ongoing processes Jerry had to engage in to move toward freedom from sexual addiction?

4. In his recovery, how did Jerry move from mere "sin management" to a transformed inner life? What disciplines do you need to engage in that will, over time, allow you to have a transformed life?

5. What is the role of the will in conjunction with the power of the Holy Spirit to gain freedom and transformation? What is the role of the spiritual disciplines as a "means of grace" in the transformation process?

JANE'S STORY

Jane grew up in a fairly conservative evangelical family. At an early age she made a profession of faith and felt that God would eventually lead her to the mission field. Unfortunately, she also grew up in a family where her worth was based on performance and her self-esteem suffered as a result. While in high school she briefly dated Randy who was popular and the quarterback of the football team. He knew the right things to say and they became sexually involved. Feeling guilt and shame, Jane ended the relationship, recommitted her life to Christ and determined that she would have a "fresh start" with God at Bible school.

In college, she met her husband, Fred. They married and eventually made it to the mission field in Africa. After the accumulation of years of successful but stressful ministry and four children, she began to feel alienated from her busy husband. Fred was always away on short-term trips for the mission, and her children became teenagers who demanded less and less of her time. Because they were in a fairly isolated area in Africa, she felt lonely and desperate for a friend. Nagging doubts about her attractiveness slowly made their way to a decision to sign up for a Facebook account. She quickly found that she had a number of "friends" and enjoyed the newly found social interaction.

Within a couple of weeks, however, she reconnected with Randy. Despite the passing years and numerous ministry experiences, it was great to reunite with someone from her past. Suddenly she felt alive, attractive and desirable. Randy still knew the right things to say and let Jane know that although he had been married and divorced twice, he had never stopped thinking about her. The memory of "the life that once was" and the fantasy of "the life that could have been" began to work overtime in Jane's mind. As time went on the tone and topics of conversation with Randy became more and more sexual.

At one point, Jane's teenage daughter discovered the dialogue on the computer and confronted her mother. Terrified, Jane promised that this was a onetime lapse in judgment and that it wouldn't happen again. Her daughter agreed to keep the secret from Dad on the condition that Mom would no longer have Facebook contact with her former boyfriend.

On a visit back to the States, she decided to visit some old friends in her hometown and decided to let Randy know that she would be willing to meet him for coffee to get caught up on old times. They had in fact continued their Internet communication for several months prior to actually meeting each other face-to-face.

The rest of the family went back to their mission station in Africa. On the day Jane was to return to Africa, she called and let the family know that she had decided not to return to the field.

When I got the call from the mission agency, Jane had abandoned her husband and four children, her ministry as a missionary and her reputation in order to resume the relationship with Randy. After all, she had "always been in love with him, and besides she and the children could still have a great relationship" even if she weren't married to their father. She told her oldest son, "I deserve to be happy for once in my life." As of this writing, the family is devastated and broken—and Mom is still with Randy. The father and children were recalled to the States for help and support and are uncertain about their future on the mission field.

Based on what you've learned in this book, can you trace the "broken windows" and steps of decline for both Jane and Fred? Think through the answers to the following questions:

1. What issues did Jane not deal with as a teen that left her susceptible to advances by Randy?

2. What were some of the triggers in Jane's life that led to her fall into sexual sin?

3. If Jane were to return to the family, what changes would Jane and Fred need to make?

4. Considering the steps outlined in this book, how would Jane need to deal with Randy?

5. What spiritual disciplines would you suggest that both Jane and Fred engage in to reconnect their lives to one another and to God?

6. What specific steps of confession, repentance, safeguards, accountability and eventual spiritual transformation does Jane need to take to restore her relationship with her husband? With her children?

Endnotes

Chapter 1

1. James Q. Wilson and George L. Kelling, "Broken Windows," *Atlantic Monthly* (March 1982): 29.

2. Malcolm Gladwell, "The Tipping Point," *The New Yorker*, June 3, 1996. Online at http://www.gladwell.com/1996/1996_06_03_a_tipping.htm

3. See John Carlin, "How They Cleaned Up Precinct 75," *The Independent* (January 7, 1996). Cited in Charles Colson, *The Christian in Today's Culture* (Wheaton, IL: Tyndale, 1999, 2001), Chapter 7.

4. See George L. Kelling and Catherine M. Coles, *Fixing Broken Windows: Restoring Order and Reducing Crime in Our Communities* (New York: Free Press, 1996), 55–56.

5. An example of how "Broken Windows" theory has been implemented in a community is found in Gwinnet County, GA: "Operation Fix-

ing Broken Windows." The author notes how "business and neighborhood groups, civic clubs, churches and other organizations join with county government to help clean up eyesores, enforce laws and regulations, and encourage everyone who lives, works, or owns property here to take pride in our community." Online at www.co.gwinnett.ga.us.

6. As an example of its widespread use, "Broken Windows" theory was applied as a "zero tolerance" policy in a boarding school setting at St. Stithian Boys College in South Africa. See www.stithian.com/webs/bcollege/admin/newsletter No. 6, September 8, 2000.

7. For an example of "Broken Windows" in a business setting, see Michael Levine, *Broken Windows, Broken Business: How the Smallest Remedies Reap the Biggest Rewards* (New York: Warner Books, 2006).

8. See Edwin J. Feulner's commencement speech at Hillsdale College, May 2004, "Lay Your Hammer Down: The Incivility of Our Times." Feulner cites the "Broken Windows" of civility in relationships. Reprinted from *Imprimus*, the nationwide speech digest of Hillsdale College.

9. Colson, *The Christian in Today's Culture*, Chapter 7, 127.

10. Ibid, 132.

CHAPTER 2

1. "Statistics on Pornography, Sexual Addition and Online Perpetrators," *Safe Families* (February

22, 2008). Online at http://www.safefamilies.org/sfStats.php.

2. Stan Donaldson, "Promise Keepers Promise to Do Better," *Plain Dealer,* September 7, 2008, B1, 6.

3. Devon Williams, "Friday Five: Jason Carroll," February 29, 2008. Online at http://www.citizenlink.org/content/AOOOOO6685.cfm.

4. Ramona Richards, *Today's Christian Woman,* online at http://www.christianitytoday.com/tcw/2003/005/5.58html.

5. C. Peter Wagner, *Prayer Shield* (Ventura, CA: Regal Books, 1992), 64.

6. *Leadership,* Winter 2006. Online at www.leadershipjournal.net.

7. Bob Russell, *When God Builds a Church* (West Monroe, LA: Howard Publishing, 2000), 74–75.

8. "Wife Says Haggard Told Her of Struggles Years Ago," Associated Press, January 27, 2009. Online at http://apnews.myway.com//article/20090127/D95VNC080.html.

9. John W. Kennedy, *Christianity Today,* March 2008. Online at http://www.christianitytoday.com/ct/article_printhtml.

10. N2H2 Internet Filtering Company.

11. Online at www.Boutell.com.

12. Bruce Wilkerson, *Set Apart* (Sisters, OR: Multnomah, 2003), 139.

13. "Is Pornography Truly a Victimless Crime?: Portions of Ted Bundy's Execution interview with James Dobson," February 15, 2009. Online at http://www.geocities.com/campuschristians_sjc/articles/bundyinterview.html.

14. Jeff Merron, "This Bud's For You," February 15, 2009. Online at http://espn.go.com/page2/s/list/partyanimals.html.

15. Terry Crist, *Learning the Language of Babylon* (Orlando: Xulon Press, 2004), 38.

CHAPTER 3

1. A.T. Robertson, *Word Pictures in the New Testament*, vol. 4. (Grand Rapids, MI: Baker, 1931), 122.

2. William Shakespeare, *Julius Caesar*, Act 4, Scene 3.

3. W.J. Townsend, H.B. Workman and George B. Eayrs, *New History of Methodism* (Nashville: Methodist Episcopal Church, South, 1909), 63.

CHAPTER 4

1. For more technical information related to the structure and characteristics of glass, see Louis A. Bloomfield, *How Everything Works: Making Physics out of the Ordinary* (Hoboken, NJ: Wiley, 2007), Chapter 17, 574.

2. See Dr. Richard Dobbins, *Caring for the Family of God: Surviving Life's Storms. Surviving Addiction to Pornography* (Akron, OH: EMERGE Ministries, 2000), 6.

3. See Dallas Willard, *The Divine Conspiracy* (New York: HarperCollins, 1998), especially chapter 9, for an excellent description of how to break the bondage to the "Sin in Our Body."

4. See "The Science Behind Pornography Addiction" (November 18, 2004, 2 PM SR 253). Web-

cast of congressional hearing online at http://commerce.senate.gov/live.ram. Includes testimony examining brain science related to pornography addiction and the effects of such addiction on families and communities.

5. Ibid.

6. See "Ecclesiastical Guidelines for Helping Ministers Affected by Pornography," *Enrichment* (Fall 2005): 61.

7. Special thanks to Dr. Richard Serbin and Dr. Richard D. Dobbins of EMERGE Ministries for early work on items included in these scales.

8. Patrick Carnes. "Internet Sex Screening Test." To be part of the study, log on to SexHelp.com. You will be shown the percentage that others have said "True" to the same items you indicated were "True" in your life.

CHAPTER 5

1. Anthony Lee, "Triple-Pane Windows—Saving More of Your Energy," online at http://www.replacement-windows-n-shutters.com/30373-triple-pane-window.html.

2. Thanks to Mr. Jim McDonald of Meeting God in Missions for many of the ideas in this chapter.

3. We will discuss the dynamics of this relationship much more thoroughly in chapter 8, when we describe how to integrate spiritual disciplines into the fabric of our lives.

4. Model developed by EMERGE Ministries, Inc.

5. Special thanks to Dr. Richard D. Dobbins and the Clinical Team of EMERGE Ministries for developing early versions of the "Old Self/New Self" model which makes practical the truths described in 1 Corinthians 10:13.

Chapter 6

1. Robert E. Logan and Neil Cole, *Raising Leaders for the Harvest* (St. Charles, IL: Church Smart Resources, 1995), 3–23.

2. Robert E. Logan and Neil Cole, *Raising Leaders for the Harvest* (St. Charles, IL: Church Smart Resources, 1995), Audio Tape 3.

3. EMERGE Ministries, "Just Between You and Me" card (Akron, Ohio, 2007). Thanks to Dr. M. Wayne Benson for early work on this too.

4. Donald Miller, *Blue Like Jazz* (Nashville: Thomas Nelson, 2003), 18.

5. Darren Mitchell, e-mail to the author, December 21, 2008.

Chapter 7

1. Friedrich Nietzche, *Beyond Good and Evil,* trans. Helen Zimmern (London: 1907), Section 188, 106–109.

Chapter 8

1. From the dedicatory preface to Jeremy Taylor's *Holy Living and Holy Dying: Together with Prayers, Containing the Whole Duty of a Christian,* etc. (1650; reprint, London: Henry G. Bohn, 1858) as cited in Appendix I of Dallas Willard's *The Spir-*

it of the Disciplines.

2. See Willard, *Divine Conspiracy*, chapter 9 for a more complete discussion on the "Curriculum for Christlikeness." Willard takes the discussion further with his sequel, *Renovation of the Heart* (Colorado Springs, CO: NavPress, 2002).

3. Willard, *Divine Conspiracy*, 320.

4. Ibid., 343–345.

5. See Donald S. Whitney, *Spiritual Disciplines for the Christian Life* (Colorado Springs, CO: NavPress, 1991). Whitney describes a number of spiritual disciplines and practical suggestions for cultivating them on a long-term basis.

6. See Richard J. Foster, *Celebration of Discipline* (San Francisco: Harper and Row, 1978, 1988, 1998, 2008).

7. See Dallas Willard, *The Spirit of the Disciplines* (New York: Harper and Row, 1988), ix.

8. Malcolm Gladwell, *The Tipping Point* (Boston: Little, Brown and Company, 2000), ix.

9. John Piper, "Gutsy Guilt," October 19, 2007. Online at http://www.christianitytoday.com/ct/2007/october/38.72.html.

10. C.J. Mahaney and Robin Boisvert, *This Great Salvation: Unmerited Favor, Unmatched Joy* (Gaithersburg, MD: Sovereign Grace Ministries, 1992), 20-21.

11. See the General Introduction to *The Renovare Spiritual Formation Bible* (San Francisco: HarperCollins, 2005), from which these comments are summarized.

ALSO BY ARNOLD R. FLEAGLE

Planted by the Water

First Peter Commentary

Journey to Bethlehem with Timothy Botts

Foundations I

Foundations II

Developing Your Secret Closet of Prayer
with Richard Burr

Knowing Jesus (Editor and writer, 2000)

Psalms for the Seasons of Life

The authors may be contacted for speaking
engagements at the following e-mails:
Dr. Arnold Fleagle: afleagle@centurytel.net
Dr. Donald Lichi: dlichi@emerge.org